In a social media world where memes are more influential than mentors, it's sometimes difficult to resist the lies of culture. Words matter and ideas have consequences. Let Alisa Childers help you differentiate between current thinking and correct theology. *Live Your Truth and Other Lies* will change the way you think about the claims of culture and their impact on your life.

> **J. WARNER WALLACE**, *Dateline*-featured cold-case detective, senior fellow at the Colson Center for Christian Worldview, and author of *Cold-Case Christianity* and *Person of Interest*

This book is a kind but firm corrective to the nice-sounding lies so often peddled today. We are told to find our own truth, to put ourselves first, to trust ourselves. Alisa Childers charts a better way through her story, cultural examples, humor, and most importantly, biblical truth.

> **DOUGLAS GROOTHUIS**, professor of philosophy at Denver Seminary and author of *Christian Apologetics*, second edition

Relatable, funny, and enlightening! Through personal stories, research, and practical application, Alisa offers insight into how lies have affected our day-to-day lives without our even knowing it. Best of all, she provides simple truth from the Bible to combat this self-obsessed stressful culture.

> **JOHN L. COOPER**, lead singer of Skillet, author of *Awake and Alive to Truth*, and host of the *Cooper Stuff Podcast*

In her own relational style, Alisa gives us a window into the lies of our culture by showing how easily we are deceived when we follow our own opinions rather than the Bible's description of our need and its remedy. Through personal experience and the lens of Scripture, she helps us see how we need to return to the Owner's Manual, the God who created us and instructs us for our own good and for his own glory. This book is immensely readable but also immensely helpful in pointing us to the source of truth. Read this book and give it to someone who is being swayed by the believable but deceptive lies that we confront daily in this information age.

**DR. ERWIN W. LUTZER**, pastor emeritus of Moody Church, Chicago

Alisa Childers is a gift to this generation. She teaches the gospel with wisdom and clarity while confronting cultural lies with the unchanging truth of God's Word. *Live Your Truth and Other Lies* will compel you to know what you believe and why you believe it, challenging you to live counterculturally for Christ.

**GRETCHEN SAFFLES**, bestselling author of *The Well-Watered Woman* and founder of Well-Watered Women

# Live Your Truth and Other Lies

# LIVE YOUR TRUTH

and *Other Lies*

**Exposing Popular Deceptions That Make Us
Anxious, Exhausted, and Self-Obsessed**

## Alisa Childers

TYNDALE
MOMENTUM®

*A Tyndale nonfiction imprint*

Visit Tyndale online at www.tyndale.com.

Visit Tyndale Momentum online at www.tyndalemomentum.com.

Visit Alisa Childers at alisachilders.com.

*Tyndale*, Tyndale's quill logo, *Tyndale Momentum*, and the Tyndale Momentum logo are registered trademarks of Tyndale House Ministries. Tyndale Momentum is a nonfiction imprint of Tyndale House Publishers, Carol Stream, Illinois.

*Live Your Truth and Other Lies: Exposing Popular Deceptions That Make Us Anxious, Exhausted, and Self-Obsessed*

Published in association with the literary agency of William K. Jensen Literary Agency, 119 Bampton Court, Eugene, OR 97404.

For information about special discounts for bulk purchases, please contact Tyndale House Publishers at csresponse@tyndale.com, or call 1-855-277-9400.

**Library of Congress Cataloging-in-Publication Data**

A catalog record for this book is available from the Library of Congress.

ISBN 978-1-4964-5566-6

Printed in the United States of America

28   27   26   25   24   23   22
7    6    5    4    3    2    1

For my husband, Mike,

who has never wavered from Truth

# CONTENTS

# AIRPLANES

Trust Me . . . Even Though I've Never Done This Before

No caress is sweeter than your charity and no
love is more rewarding than the love of your
truth, which shines in beauty above all else.

Saint Augustine, *Confessions*

My finger was literally on the button. Everything in me wanted to click Like and Share. *Why am I not doing it?* I thought. The author of the meme was a Christian, the quote sounded positive and life-affirming, and it would surely encourage and uplift my social media friends. *I still can't do it. But why?* With my index finger lightly tapping the top of the computer mouse, I sat pondering my hesitation. Then, in a sudden burst of clarity, the Holy Spirit was all like, "Snap out of it!" *Oh yeah.* I was hesitating because although this quote sounded nice, *it was not biblical.* It was actually *a lie . . .* a happy little lie.

Have you ever found yourself in a similar spot? I can't tell you how many times I've checked social media only to see a message like "Follow your heart." And I'm thinking, *Awww. That's nice.* I hit Like before I have a chance to remember, *Oh, wait. The last time I followed my heart it got smashed to bits and took me years of counseling to recover.* "Trust your instincts. They never lie." That one landed me in traffic court.

What if those little slogans that sound positive and life-affirming are really just lies that will unhinge us from truth, reality, and hope? Relying on popular wisdom can cause unnecessary pain and confusion. In other cases, it leads to absolute bondage to whatever virtue signal of the day is dominating the internet. Are you tired of feeling like you have to check social media to find out what you're supposed to think? Are you weary of the latest self-help book that promises to set you free but only imprisons you with a laundry list of studies to consider, positive affirmations to recite, Facebook groups to join, causes to advocate for, and other books to read? (It seems as if it were really "self-help," I shouldn't need all this outside support!)

In that moment of hesitation over a meme, I realized that there are endless ways truth can be spun, manipulated, covered up, and even used to promote deception. Often, the lie is christened with religious language, so the temptation to share it without thinking is real. As A. W. Tozer said, "Too much of contemporary Christianity is borrowed from the philosophies of the world and even other religions—phrases and mottos that on the surface look great but are not rooted in Scripture or that mostly bolster one's self-image."[1]

These happy little lies are pithy assertions that sound good, safe, optimistic, and constructive. They look great stitched on a pillow, digitized into a meme, or turned into a slogan. They are usually stated in a positive form, like "Believe in yourself" and "You are perfect just as you are." You see, the best lies are the ones that sound the most beautiful. They are made up of at least 50 percent truth. Sometimes they are almost totally true. But that small bit that spins the entire outcome? That is the important part.

Our culture is brimming with slogans that promise peace, fulfillment, freedom, empowerment, and hope. These messages have become such an integral component of our American consciousness that many people don't even think to question them. They sound nice and carry an illusion of truth. Often these messages are popularized by social media celebrities who claim to be Christians, promote their materials as being in agreement with Christian principles, and publish on Christian platforms and venues.

The problem? They are lies.

## NEWBIE

More than ever before, people are looking to their own hearts, opinions, preferences, biases, and predispositions to guide them through life. In other words, we have learned to trust our feelings. But how is that working out for us? It is leading to all sorts of problems. And in so many cases . . . didn't we get *ourselves* into this mess in the first place?

Today we have authors, influencers, and life-coach gurus peddling their personal transformation stories as models for others to follow. Their advice is frequently based on very recent life-altering decisions that seem to make them happy in the moment but have not stood the test of time. In some cases, their books come out within a few months of a major life change, divorce, paradigm shift in identity, or spiritual deconstruction, which they think helped them discover their true selves. Often their instructions include throwing out thousands of years of wisdom (ahem . . . the Bible) and hundreds of faithful and godly Bible teachers (*Elisabeth Elliot? What a prude. Charles Spurgeon? Ugh . . . what a drag*) and replacing them with something (or someone) they decided to try literally five minutes ago. And we are supposed to follow these people? Reader. Listen. Please do not take life advice from someone who is in the middle of a major crisis. Unless they are gleaning from time-tested, biblical wisdom and pointing you to Christ (not yourself), it would be wise to hit the pause button on that hot mess and just wait and see how it all pans out over the next ten years or so.

Taking advice from someone because they're funny, self-confident, or Instagram savvy makes me think of a hypothetical scenario in the air. First, you should know that I've been on more airplanes than I can count. In fact, on early-morning flights, I can fall asleep on any plane, in any seat, in any row. I've practically got it down to a science. Before take-off, I unpack my neck pillow, insert my earplugs, and cover my eyes with the top of my hoodie, lacing it up tight. With my head tilted back and just my nose and mouth peeking out of the hoodie hole, I'm usually in snooze-ville by the time the plane takes off. If I don't wake up until landing, I consider it a personal victory. If none of my traveling buddies throws a

Cheez-It into my unconsciously wide-open mouth—double victory.

Obviously, I don't tend to get nervous about flying. I sleep like a baby. Maybe this is because I have flown so frequently, or maybe it's because I've got other things on my mind. Mainly I think it's because I know that the training pilots go through is rigorous . . . especially when it comes to commercial flying, where the lives of so many citizens are at stake. At the end of the day, I trust the airline industry to keep me safe.

But imagine I step on a plane and just after takeoff the pilot announces, "Good morning, everyone. I'd like to thank you for joining me on my very first flight ever. Not to worry, I've spent quite a few hours in classroom education and flight simulators. Oh, and our copilot couldn't make it this morning, but I feel confident I'll do a great job and get you all to your destination safely and on time." Can you imagine the level of anxiety that would strike the heart of every passenger in that moment? That's because *trust* is a huge part of feeling safe and secure.

But what and whom can we trust when it comes to knowledge about life, death, goodness, and purpose? I don't think it's an exaggeration to say that our culture has never been more divided, polarized, or suspicious. No one knows where they can find reliable information about anything from brownie recipes to personal health to morality to politics. Depression and anxiety are skyrocketing, especially among young people.[2]

I don't know about you, but I find that relying on whatever the loudest and most attractive voices say is true on a given day is absolutely exhausting. In many cases, these voices are like that brand-new airline pilot announcing to the passengers that he's never really done this before, but they should definitely trust him with their lives. It's like, "Hi, I'm a self-help guru who keeps making really bad decisions and many of my relationships are in shambles. But I'm super authentic about it, so you should for sure let me be your life coach."

## HOW TO BUILD A FIRM FOUNDATION

Reader, I'm going to make a bold claim. I think that ditching the jargon and clinging to the timeless truths of the Bible is the most freeing and stabilizing thing we can do. It will ease anxiety, quell depression, and calm a restless heart. Recognizing who we are in Christ is the ultimate self-care because the Word of God doesn't reinvent itself along with a constantly changing culture. In fact, you should know at the outset that I wrote this book with the assumption that the Bible is authoritative for our lives. My first book, *Another Gospel?*, explains the evidence I discovered for staking my life on Scripture after my own faith was severely shaken. The short version is this: Scripture has stood the test of thousands of years, been endorsed by millions who have been transformed by its truth, and given countless believers a solid foundation for knowing God and living out their faith. We have good evidence from history, archaeology, and biblical scholarship to trust that we have an accurate copy and that what it records is true. Jesus told us in Matthew 24:35 that his words will never pass away. We know from Hebrews 13:8

that Jesus is the same yesterday, today, and forever. He doesn't change, and his words will remain forever. To put it another way, I believe the Bible is the Word of God because that was Jesus' view. I am a Jesus follower, and my beliefs reflect what he taught.

In Matthew 7:24, he says, "Everyone then who hears these words of mine and does them will be like a wise man who built his house on the rock." He goes on to explain that rain and floods can't wash that house away, and winds can't blow it down no matter how hard it gets bombarded. On the other hand, Jesus says that whoever hears his words and doesn't do them is like a foolish man who built his house on sand. Where are Jesus' words recorded? In the New Testament. And what does Jesus say in the New Testament about the rest of the Bible? He continually refers to the Old Testament Scriptures as the "Word of God." He also claims to *actually be* the God of the Old Testament, so in that sense, there really is no such thing as "red letters" in the Bible. They are all red letters. Jesus is God, and God inspired Scripture "for teaching, for reproof, for correction, and for training in righteousness" (2 Timothy 3:16). As followers of Jesus, shouldn't we take him at his word?[3]

In many ways, this is a book about the Bible. It's also a book about logic and common sense and the ridiculous ways we talk ourselves out of those things. Mostly, though, it's a book about planting our feet on the bedrock of God's truth . . . truth that doesn't evolve with cultural trends. As a wise friend once said to me, "I'd rather have a shack on solid ground than a mansion on the sand."

In the next chapter, we'll consider some critical reasons it's so easy to become confused today—the changing nature of language and the tendency to focus on ourselves. In each chapter after that, we will examine a popular deception and compare that lie with what the Bible says. Then, reader, you will have a choice to make. Will you choose to stand on the unchanging truth of the God-breathed Scriptures, or will you choose whatever trendy catchphrase people are currently obsessed with? The choice is yours.

As for me and my house? We choose to build on the rock. We choose peace. We choose hope. We choose to live *the* truth.

## 2

# TROUSERS

Rebuilding the Tower of Babel—or Is It "Babble"?

"Anyone can ask questions," said Mr. Wonka.
"It's the answers that count."

Roald Dahl, *Charlie and the Great Glass Elevator*

I once told a British Christian rock star I liked his underwear. Well, I didn't *mean* to tell him that. I meant to tell him he was wearing very nice pants. But what I didn't know at the time was that in England, some words have different meanings than they do in America.

In anticipation of my singing group ZOEgirl's first album release, I was invited to fly across the pond to attend a party in honor of a successful rock band that had enjoyed a string of hits in the US. We would meet over tea and scones dotted with Devonshire cream, and it would all be just so fancy. By the time I arrived, this steadfast introvert was already nervous about all the upcoming social interaction. There would be mingling, small talk, and uncomplicated questions . . . the trifecta of my greatest nightmare.

Our luxury town car (did I mention everything was fancy?) pulled up to a small recording studio that seemed to be the only building for miles along the lush, green English countryside. My anxiety grew as I realized I would have to actually *talk to these people*. This band had quite literally orchestrated the soundtrack of my young adult life, and I had no idea what to say when I met them.

Am I the only introvert who concocts avoidance plans at parties? Mine goes something like this. First, I walk in and find a bathroom. Second, I go into the bathroom and stay there for a minute to scope things out and plan my next move. Then I peek out from behind the bathroom door and look around for some kind of dessert table or coffee station. Next, I proceed to said table and take a ridiculously long time pouring the coffee and perusing the desserts. Hopefully by then I will have pep-talked myself into putting on my big girl pants and just being a grown-up human already. But not this time. My avoidance plan was thwarted immediately because the lead singer was right there when I walked through the front door. There was nothing between us but a table of pastries and finger sandwiches.

Starstruck and stunned, I was unable to come up with something a normal person might say, so I blurted out, "I like your pants!" (In my defense, they were very posh velvet bell-bottoms that screamed Mick Jagger circa 1971.) His eyes widened and a pitying smile crawled across his face as I realized I had made a terrible mistake. "Trousers," he said. "We call them trousers." He was very gracious about it. But now that I had accidentally harassed my favorite Christian singer,

I was going to have to quit my job and move to Canada, obviously.

In that moment I realized that words and their context are critical components of communication. What I understood as *outerwear*, he understood as *underwear*. Pants: one word, two very different concepts. But you don't even have to live on two different continents for miscommunication to happen.

## WORD SALAD

With words constantly evolving in definition and meaning, these types of mix-ups can happen even among people who grew up on the same street. For example, take the word *tolerance*. Years ago, tolerance meant that even though you might disagree with someone else's opinion, you respected their right to say it and wouldn't retaliate with violence or abuse. However, that is not what most people mean when they use the word today. In our culture, tolerance often means celebrating and affirming the opinion of someone else and never implying that they could be objectively wrong about anything—especially when it comes to morality or religion. But this modern usage of tolerance is not just a redefinition; it is the exact opposite of what the word *actually* means. You can't tolerate a person unless you disagree with them! This updated definition robs people of having actual opinions . . . at least ones they are permitted to say out loud. When writing about the seven deadly sins, English writer Dorothy Sayers notes that another word for the deadly sin of sloth (apathy) is tolerance:

> In the world it calls itself tolerance; but in hell it is
> called despair . . . the sin that believes in nothing, cares
> for nothing, seeks to know nothing, interferes with
> nothing, enjoys nothing, loves nothing, hates nothing,
> finds purpose in nothing, lives for nothing, and remains
> alive only because there is nothing it would die for.[1]

But *tolerance* isn't the only word getting a modern-day makeover. Words like *love, hate, bigot, male, female, oppression, justice,* and *truth*—many of which we'll talk about in this book—are all being constantly refashioned. So you can imagine the confusion that can happen when people don't carefully define their terms. We can end up talking past each other, never coming to an agreeable conclusion simply because we aren't thinking about what our words mean.

In *Mama Bear Apologetics: Empowering Your Kids to Challenge Cultural Lies,* Hillary Morgan Ferrer refers to this phenomenon as "linguistic theft," which she defines as "*purposefully hijacking words, changing their definitions, and then using those same words as tools of propaganda.*"[2] I would add that in some cases, linguistic theft takes place unintentionally. When we fail to be careful with our words, they can morph and change in their usage, and we can subconsciously adopt a whole new vocabulary without even realizing it. Ferrer identifies five ways that linguistic theft undermines real communication:

1. It can stop a conversation in its tracks. (Just accuse your ideological opponent of "hate speech," and the discussion is over.)

2. It can cause people to act before thinking an issue all the way through. (Forget about waiting for all the facts to come in . . . jump on whatever virtue-signaling bandwagon Twitter is on today so you don't get canceled!)

3. It obscures the specifics. (Who needs to investigate what a particular organization believes and funds as long as it *sounds* like a good cause?)

4. It assumes the worst of opponents. (Think Twitter in 2020, where everyone you disagreed with thought you were "literally Hitler.")

5. Finally, it presents a negative as a positive, or a positive as a negative. (Think about the terms *pro-choice* and *reproductive justice*. They sound nice, right? They are positive phrases used to shield people from the horrifying reality of abortion and make them feel virtuous for their proabortion activism.)[3]

## BABEL OR BABBLE?

These are just a few examples of the complicated relationship we humans have with language. It reminds me of a certain Bible story we all grew up hearing.

"Now the whole earth had one language and the same words," Genesis 11:1 tells us. A long time ago, people thought they were pretty big stuff, so they migrated from the east, built a city, and began constructing a tower with the goal of reaching the heavens. But this skyscraper wasn't born out of a humble pursuit of worshiping God. Those assembling it had the goal of becoming their own gods. "Let us make a name for ourselves," they said (verse 4). But God was all like, "Not today, Satan." So he confused their language and scattered them all over the world (verses 7-8). And just like that, their little building project was abandoned.

They wanted to make a name for themselves because they were afraid that they would be "dispersed over the face of the whole earth" (verse 4). Ironically, that is exactly what ended up happening. But why would God blame them for finding one another, living and working in peace and unity, communicating perfectly, and setting life goals that would make Elon Musk seem like a lazy bum? I hate to be the bearer of bad news, but peace and unity are not always the highest virtues.

You see, the problem at Babel wasn't that people were so good at working well with others. It's that they were working well with others *for nefarious purposes*. It's kind of like when my children were younger and they once had peace with each other for fifteen whole minutes. They disappeared into a bedroom and the house went quiet. I hardly knew what to do with the "me time" their little unity session allowed for. Before I could figure it out, they reemerged having used a Sharpie to create designs on one another's faces before filling in the shapes with paint that was now smeared into their hair and clothing. Needless to say, I busted out the soap before dispersing them to two different locations in the house. Who knows what they could have accomplished with more time, resources, and expert communication skills? Much like the parent who separates mischievous children, God separated people for their own good.

But we never learn, do we? We now seem to be resuming our age-old building project. In ancient times they used bricks and mortar. Today we use computers, smartphones, and social media to try to bring the world together. Different materials—same results. However, instead of a tower to heaven, we have created an online society and mass media distribution system that's proliferating sexual immorality, self-worship, discord, and misinformation, with armchair prophets teaching every sort of falsehood.

And still our language is confused. We talk past each other, define words differently, value knowledge and meaning in different ways, shun logic, and celebrate all viewpoints as equally valid (except traditional Christian ones). It's as if we've been scattered and confused like the post-Babel world, while still being together in the same chaotic pre-Babel online and printed space. This is why it has never been more difficult to live as a person dedicated to truth. If we are going to be truth seekers, we will have to be purposeful and intentional, with thick skin as tough as nails.

The power of the social media platform is a modern echo of an ancient error. Although social media can certainly do a lot of good, the phenomenon has also given birth to a myriad of self-made Bible teachers and bloggers who shepherd millions of followers. Many of these personalities have drifted into progressive Christianity and are now leading their flocks away from the historic gospel. In fact, my own faith crisis occurred when I took a special class from the pastor at my former church, who was questioning Christian doctrine at the time. Thankfully, over several years God rebuilt my faith as I studied arguments for his existence and the truthfulness of Christianity, examined church history, read classics from the early church fathers, and learned directly from experts in biblical scholarship and Scripture.

I've come to realize that the bestselling books, podcasts, and blogs by those who have left historic Christianity behind preach a "gospel" of self. In fact, so many of the lies we will cover in this book begin with the foundation of self: To be authentic I must belong to myself. To be happy I must put myself first. To be fulfilled I must be enough for myself. To be successful I must control my own destiny. All these ideas build upon the starting point of self. But as we look at each lie, we'll see *the self* is a faulty foundation. It's a structure with cracks in it. It's broken. Anything we build upon it will be vulnerable to the current positive affirmation that sounds right to us in the moment. At best, this can send us on fruitless searches for meaning. At worst, it can propel us into ruin. This is why it's so vital for Christians to ensure that our foundation is Christ, not ourselves.

Live your truth versus live *the* truth. It's a big difference.

The call to be true only to one's own feelings and desires is the exact opposite of the teachings of Jesus and the historic Christian faith. It's easy to point people to themselves. There will always be a market for that. We love it! We love to talk about ourselves, focus on ourselves, pamper ourselves, and adore ourselves. It all has to do with that pesky sin nature thing we'll talk about in chapter 4. But we were not created to worship ourselves. We were created with a different purpose . . . to glorify God and enjoy him forever.[4] Anything that distracts us from that will not make us happy. God is our Creator, and he knows what will truly bring us peace, joy, and happiness. And guess what? It's not a mirror or a selfie stick. It's him.

Understanding our purpose as humans will require us to commit ourselves to absolute truth. We will have to learn critical thinking skills and examine carefully what our words mean. But it will also require us to do some unlearning. We must learn to rethink what we have been indoctrinated with ever since singing along with *The Little Mermaid* as she finally got her legs, her prince, and everything she ever dreamed of. I love Disney movies as much as anyone, but Ariel triumphed after she disobeyed her dad and decided to live her truth. That's one heck of a confusing message to send to people who don't yet have fully developed frontal lobes. After all, as we'll soon discover, "your truth" is as mythical as King Triton's magical trident and the kingdom of merfolk he and Ariel come from.

# 3

# LEPRECHAUNS

## Live Your Truth

You can choose what you believe, Shuffler,
but you can't change what's true.

S. D. Smith, *The Green Ember*

"Lepwechauns are weal, Mom."

I stared into the earnest brown eyes of my smart-as-a-whip daughter as she made her opening remarks for what our household now solemnly refers to as "the great leprechaun debate of 2013." There was bitter disagreement. There were tears. There were arguments and rebuttals. Evidence and refutations. It was practically Armageddon. At four and a half, my analytical offspring was convinced that a leprechaun had visited her classroom, and she would not be persuaded otherwise.

I was a bit surprised to hear this because generally you can't pull one over on her. I mean, this is the woman-child who upon discovering her first loose tooth sat me down and informed me the tooth fairy isn't real. She said, "I know the moms do it, and I want to know if I can just have toys instead of money." (Turns out the tooth fairy in our neighborhood is terribly forgetful and should be fired immediately. So that little arrangement worked out just fine.) Plus, my daughter had asked me only the week before if leprechauns exist. I assured her they were fictional characters contained within storybooks and nothing more. I thought we'd moved on.

We had *not* moved on. It turns out her preschool teacher thought it would be fun to make the kids think a leprechaun had snuck into their classroom overnight to decorate for Saint Patrick's Day. My daughter arrived at school the next morning to discover green streamers hung from doorframes, construction paper shamrocks pinned to bulletin boards, and clover-colored balloons fastened to the backs of chairs. "Oh my goodness! What's going on?" her teacher exclaimed in fabricated surprise. When the kids were unable to figure out where all the festive ornamentation came from, the teacher "found" a little black buckled shoe in front of the exit door. "How did *this* get here?" she asked the children, who collectively came to the same conclusion: a leprechaun. Mystery solved.

My daughter came straight home and made her big announcement. Leprechauns were, in fact, a thing . . . and everyone just needed to get on board with this new reality. Not wanting to burst her bubble, I gently asked, "How do you know that?"

She replied, "Because a leprechaun decorated our classroom during the night!"

"Hmm," I responded. "And how do you know it was a leprechaun?"

She came right back with, "My teacher found his shoe that fell off while he was making his escape!"

"Okay. But sweetie, do you remember when I told you they weren't real?"

"Yes! But I saw the shoe! And . . . he left *gold dust* behind."

"Gold dust?"

"GOLD DUST."

"Okay, listen," I responded. "I think someone might be making this up."

"No. Lepwechauns are weal, Mom."

I let it go for the moment, thinking she would forget about it and move on to something more pressing, like Santa Claus. But no. Not my daughter. They say some children are born with old souls. My daughter was about forty-seven when she was born (not in a mystical reincarnation kind of way but in a "wise beyond her years" sense). I've been trying to catch up with her ever since. When she believes something is true, she is as serious as death. My curly-haired, ribbon-clad forensic investigator went off to school the next day like she'd been hired by *20/20* to blow the lid off the whole "leprechauns don't exist" conspiracy theory. After school, she marched through the door, reached into her little navy-blue sweater pocket, and produced a handful of gold glitter. There it was. The shiny, glimmering, sparkly proof. And there was nothing I could do to convince her she had been duped.

It wasn't until a couple of years later that she admitted she might have been wrong about the existence of leprechauns. It took some time and life experience for her mind to accept the truth . . . that it was all a lie. A happy little lie. Think about it. A four-year-old with grand ideas and glittered proof—what more did she need to establish her reality?

If we are honest with ourselves, aren't we the same? Don't we tend to start with what we find compelling and beautiful and then seek only the sources that prove our preconceived understanding of the way the world is? But the reality is, truth is true no matter how we feel about it.

Leprechauns either exist or they don't. It doesn't matter how strongly my daughter felt about their existence, or how strongly I felt about their nonexistence. She could shout "her truth" about leprechauns from the top of the social media tower in the sky, but it wouldn't change reality.

## POSTMODERNISM'S SECRET LOVE CHILD

Sometime during the upheaval that was 2020, black signs with brightly colored ink started to pop up on lawns all around the country. It was as if a new moral creed had been codified and canonized in the American suburban consciousness. When taken at face value, all the statements seemed right and good. Love *is* love. Women's rights *are* human rights. Science *is* real . . . and so on. But what many people didn't realize is that a few of the words used in this new creed had been linguistically stolen and repurposed as slogans for certain causes. According to this creed (and contrary to 1 Corinthians 13), *love is love* means affirming virtually any sexual relationship someone wants to engage in. *Women's rights* means helping to keep abortion legal. *No human is illegal* is a way of advocating for specific immigration policies. Whether or not you agree with those sentiments is irrelevant. The point is that the words were being redefined right under our noses.

How did this happen? We can thank the 1960s for producing a philosophy that became incredibly trendy over the next couple of decades, then sort of fizzled out, mutated and came back on the scene, and is now on the throne of popular thinking. The philosophy is called postmodernism, and it has infected nearly every facet of our lives, especially how we think and process information. Postmodernism questions many of the concepts that define modernity, like democracy, the scientific age, reason, and individual liberties. It's deeply skeptical of objective truth and suspicious of the power dynamics of those who claim to know it. In other words, according to postmodernism, if objective truth exists, no one can claim to know it absolutely. If they say they do, it's most likely a power grab. I think it's fair to sum up postmodern thought with the slogan, "What's true for you is true for you, but what's true for me is true for me." Live and let live.

In the 1960s, French philosopher Jacques Derrida gave birth to postmodernism's love child, a phenomenon called deconstruction. For Derrida, deconstruction had to do with how text and meaning are related to one another. He was skeptical that absolute truth could be found through language and thought that words could not be narrowed down to singular and definite meanings. In their book about the impact of postmodernism, authors Helen Pluckrose and

James Lindsay noted that in Derrida's view, "the speaker's meaning has no more authority than the hearer's interpretation and thus intention cannot outweigh impact."[1] Of course, we can't move on without noting the irony of a man who used words to communicate these ideas, which I'm sure he expected people to understand and apply according to *his* intentions.

Now we see stories of deconstruction everywhere. It seems like almost every time we open our social media news feeds, another celebrity Christian has announced that they have lost their faith. Often, these posts are followed by detailed explanations of their "deconstruction stories." In this sense, deconstruction means the slow unraveling of someone's faith as many of the beliefs they grew up with are picked apart and discarded. Although Derrida's definition of deconstruction and the current usage of the word *deconstruction* might not mean the exact same thing, I think the reason it has become such a fad is because of the postmodern influence on our collective thinking. If objective truth is viewed as nonexistent or unreachable, wouldn't it actually be virtuous to deconstruct the constructs of reality we've been handed? If words can be redefined to suit a presupposed narrative, wouldn't faith deconstruction be a natural and unavoidable reality for those who have embraced a postmodern worldview?

Much of the deconstruction we see in the context of faith happens on the level of language. Words are redefined, and precious core doctrines of the Christian faith are explained away. In many cases, *Resurrection* ceases to refer to an empty tomb and the physical appearance of Jesus after his death and becomes a metaphor for the possibility of new life after hardship or destructive tendencies. *Incarnation* no longer means God becoming flesh but rather Jesus achieving enlightenment and the mystery of the Cosmic Christ.[2] The *Atonement* no longer means Jesus dying on the cross as a sacrifice for our sins but is merely a picture of how to forgive others. Before you know it, you've lost the gospel and have redefined not just words but the entire Christian worldview. It becomes meaningless and empty, with no power to save. Deconstruction is the aftermath of the war on words.

## THOUGHT EXPERIMENTS

### 2+2=5

We live in a time and place where many people don't even know what truth is. (Thanks, postmodernism!) Some think it's just a subjective opinion or preference, much like your favorite sport, movie, or candy bar. But the definition of truth is actually quite simple: Truth is a thought, statement, or opinion that lines up with reality. That's it. If what we say, think, or believe lines up with reality, it's truth. If it doesn't, it's not.

Truth is true for all people in all places and times. It's also something you can't invent, think up, or create. It is something you *discover*. It doesn't change, no matter how much people's beliefs about it do. Truth isn't altered because of how it makes someone feel. Truth is entirely unaffected by the tone and attitude of the person professing it. A lie is still a lie even when communicated with humor and just the right amount of whimsy. For example, a big jerk can shout an obscenity-laced truth, while a sweet and funny person can convincingly state a convenient untruth.

Let's do an experiment. Think about the proposition 2+2=4. It's true on every continent, in every time period, and in every culture. It's true even if someone strongly believes it's not. (Feel free to google it—but be prepared to be sucked into the vortex of endless nonsensical ramblings about the oppressive power dynamics of mathematics.) If two rocks fall into an empty ditch in the middle of the forest, and two more rocks fall into the same ditch, there will be four rocks, even if no human is there to observe or explain it. That's just how truth works. We may not like it, but what we do or don't like has zero effect on what is actually true.

### Cookies vs. Brownies

What is the best dessert? Pie? Ice cream? Brownies? Cookies? Cake? If you chose cake *with* ice cream, you would be correct. Well, actually, it just means that you're probably a really cool person and we could be food buddies. But there's actually no "best dessert." There are only opinions of what each person *thinks* is the best dessert. That's because "best dessert" doesn't fall into the category of objective truth. The conclusion that "cake with ice cream is the best" is simply my opinion. It's my preference. It doesn't depend on anything outside of my own head. It's based on me, the subject. Sounds like a perfect opportunity to say, "This is my truth." But I would just be stating what I *believe* to be true about the best dessert. It's not even really *my truth* because it's true for everyone in all times and places that I, Alisa Childers, think cake and ice cream is the best dessert. This is why subjective truth isn't really a thing.[3]

Think about it this way. If I say, "Truth is subjective," I am contradicting myself. Why? Because the statement "Truth is subjective" is a claim about objective reality. It states that it is objectively true that truth is subjective . . . which, if that statement is true, means there's at least one objective truth . . . which means the statement is false. (It's okay to take a moment and read that last sentence a few more times.)

## TRUTH MATTERS

I know I promised this book would compare popular deceptions with what the Bible says. What the heck does this all have to do with the Bible? In this chapter, it's taken a minute to get here.

First of all, if we don't have a framework upon which to defend the idea that words have meaning and truth can be known, we might as well throw our Bibles out the window and do what we want. So there's that. But the Bible also has a lot to say about reality. In fact, Christianity is a belief system that stands or falls on objective truth. It is not simply a set of teachings, a philosophy, or a lifestyle. It's not a collection of rituals, mantras, sacraments, and affirmations. Christianity is about placing active trust in the person of Jesus and the reconciliation with God he secured for us on the Cross. All of this depends on the resurrection of Jesus being something that actually happened, an objective truth.

Here's what I mean. In the Bible, miracles—and specifically the Resurrection—are referred to as "signs." Hebrews 2:4 tells us that these signs, wonders, and various miracles were God's way of confirming or bearing witness to the message of salvation Jesus brought. Essentially, these signs serve as evidence that Christianity is true. In 1 Corinthians 15, Paul spends nearly the whole chapter defending the truthfulness of the Resurrection. He begins by saying that his purpose for writing to the Christians in Corinth is to remind them of the gospel. He passes on a creed that is about twenty years old by the time he writes this letter, in which the resurrection of Jesus is listed as one of the bedrock beliefs that define this good news that he is so eager to share. After declaring the Resurrection to be a nonnegotiable, Paul goes so far as to state that without it, our faith would be in vain. In other words, "If Christ has not been raised, your faith is futile and you are still in your sins" (verse 17).

At this point, you may be thinking that Paul is asking us to believe in a miracle that supposedly happened more than two thousand years ago just because he said it occurred. How can we know he is telling the truth? It's a fair question, and thankfully there is historical evidence in non-Christian sources that can lead us to reasonably conclude that the Resurrection actually happened. Even if you never opened a Bible, you could learn some details about Jesus' life from a number of ancient Greek, Roman, and Jewish sources within a couple of hundred years of his life.[4]

Because we have access to these ancient sources, as well as the historical accounts found in the Gospels, certain historical facts surrounding the resurrection of Jesus are virtually undisputed. Dr. Gary Habermas, a historian and New Testament scholar, is considered by many to be one of the foremost academics studying the Resurrection. He collected more than one thousand critical scholarly works on Jesus' resurrection written between 1975 and 2003. He discovered a few interesting facts that virtually every scholar—from the ultraliberal to the very conservative—agreed upon. Here are four of them:

1. Jesus died by Roman crucifixion.

2. Jesus' disciples believed he rose from the dead and appeared to them, and they were willing to suffer and die while maintaining those beliefs.

3. Church persecutor Paul suddenly became a Christian after having an experience with the one he believed to be the risen Christ.

4. James, a skeptic and brother of Jesus, suddenly converted after he believed he saw his brother raised back to life.

Habermas also noted that about three-quarters of scholars agree that Jesus' tomb was found empty.[5] You might think that atheist and skeptical Bible scholars would scoff at these historical realities, but these facts remain virtually uncontested. For example, Dr. Gerd Lüdemann, a German New Testament scholar and historian, believed that much of the New Testament is historically unreliable. Despite his skepticism, he wrote, "It may be taken as historically certain that Peter and the disciples had experiences after Jesus' death in which Jesus appeared to them as the risen Christ."[6] Likewise, famously skeptical scholar Dr. Bart Ehrman observed,

> There are two historical realities that simply cannot be denied. The followers of Jesus did claim that Jesus came back to life. If they had not claimed that, we would not have Christianity. So they did claim it. Moreover, they did claim that they knew he rose precisely because some of them saw him alive again afterward. No one can doubt that.[7]

While most scholars agree on the facts, they disagree over how to explain them. Some have tried to explain this evidence by coming up with different theories,[8] but the explanation that makes the most sense is that Jesus Christ came back to life after he was dead. As many others before me have pointed out, no one would be willing to suffer and die for what they know is a lie. Since Scripture teaches that Christianity stands or falls based on the reality of the Resurrection, can you see why it's so important to live by truth? Isn't it evident why we can't just sit back and let people redefine these words, turning them into metaphors for our best lives now? Defending the gospel requires defending objective truth. There's no way around it. Christianity is based on truth.

## LET'S COMPARE

Think about everything we've learned so far in this chapter about the nature of truth. Compare that with some more quotes from popular writers:

> When we use the language of indoctrination—with its *should* and *shouldn't*, *right* and *wrong*, *good* and *bad*— we are activating our minds. That's not what we're going for here. Because our minds are polluted by our training. In order to get beyond our training, we need to activate our imaginations. Our minds are excuse makers; our imaginations are storytellers.[9]

> I lack all objectivity. I evaluate the merit of every idea based on how it bears upon actual people.[10]

> If you feel trapped by your identity because you know it is hurting you, break free and do the work to claim the truth that fits you now. No one gets to define you but you.[11]

> To grow, to relax, to find peace, to become brave, we must witness one woman at a time doing the thing that is revolutionary for her: living her truth without asking permission or offering explanation.[12]

Notice how the author of the first quote actually instructs readers to bypass their minds—the part of their being that is responsible for assessing ideas, engaging intellectually, and discerning truth from error. Within the context of right and wrong, she encourages her audience to engage their imaginations, which isn't necessarily a bad thing—unless their imaginations are unhinged from their rational and logical minds. I'm all about the imagination (hi . . . flaky artist here), but imagination can turn dark and ugly in a hot second if it isn't grounded in truth. Can you fathom what horrors could be done if someone took this advice literally? As we'll see in the next chapter, our hearts are fallen. They lie to us and lead us astray. An imagination unhinged from objective truth is a recipe for disaster.

The second and third quotes on page 31 reflect a sentiment commonly repeated by popular thought leaders. The authors admit that they determine truth based on how it makes them or someone else feel. If a teaching makes someone feel negative, uncomfortable, or harmed, it can be deemed false and disregarded. But can you imagine if parents of small children followed this advice?

### THREE QUESTIONS TO ASK WHEN ANALYZING IDEAS

| <u>Your Truth</u> | <u>The Truth</u> |
|---|---|
| Are you being asked to bypass your mind or rational thinking? | Is this statement or situation based on objective reality? |
| Is the imagination seen as superior to and separate from your logical, rational mind? | Are you engaging your imagination while still accessing your logical, rational mind? |
| Is truth in this situation dependent on how it makes you or someone else feel? | Is truth in this situation dependent on what the Word of God says? |

## SUGAR BUGS

When my son was little, he developed a cavity in one of his back molars. The dentist informed us that he needed to wash out the "sugar bug" that had made a home in my son's sweet little chompers. When it came time to drill (I mean, wash out) said sugar bug, my son became anxious and agitated. Even though the dentist tried to smooth it over with fun words (God bless him for trying), the truth remained: There would be needles and drills and possibly some pain and discomfort. It was so difficult for me to sit there calmly as the whizzing sound of the drill reached a fever pitch and my son's eyes widened as he looked to me for rescue. But I couldn't rescue him. I knew that if we didn't deal with the cavity now, it would cause much greater decay later and lead to all sorts of health problems.

But my son didn't know this because he didn't have all the information. All he knew was that this was scary and weird and a little bit painful. I imagine that if the dentist's hands hadn't been in his mouth, my son would have cried, "Mom, why are you letting him do this to me? This doesn't feel good!" If I, as his mother, knew that this mild distress would mitigate a more significant injury, would it be loving for me to simply say, "Okay, Son. This is obviously bearing upon you negatively, so why don't you just live your truth and shun dentists. You do you"? Of course not. How much more does our heavenly Father know about the circumstances we face?

The truth is that some biblical teachings are difficult. They make us uncomfortable. They call us to deny ourselves and prefer Jesus even over our family and friends. They get all up in our sex lives, our relationships, and our identities. Contrary to the fourth quote on page 31, it's not brave or revolutionary to deny *the* truth in order to speak *your* truth. It won't help you grow, relax, or find peace. It might feel good for a while, but in the end it will simply bring anxiety, pain, depression, and exhaustion. Ultimately, it will not facilitate peace with God, which is the only true peace there is.

## HINGED

I don't think it's an exaggeration to say that there has never been a time in history in which it has been more important for us to be hinged to truth. My kids are a part of a generation called Gen Z, which is basically everyone born from the late 1990s on. A recent study concludes that most of Gen Z believes that morality changes over time. This means that the dominant view of the next generation is what is called moral relativism. When it comes to thinking about categories like right and wrong, should and shouldn't, and good and bad, most young people have adopted the cultural mantra, "Live your truth." The study also showed that Gen Z is more open to revealing their inner feelings and asking for help with their mental health than any other generation in history. At the same time, 82 percent report experiencing at least one traumatic incident,[13] with coping mechanisms ranging from connecting with friends and family to turning to digital media. Add to that the stresses of school and work, news cycles that change faster than you can blink, busy social lives, the frantic pace of the 2020s—not to mention a pandemic that muddled all those categories into one—and you have a generation that is utterly exhausted. In fact, tiredness is the most commonly reported negative emotion among this age group.

It may seem like I'm dunking on the next generation, but I actually have a lot of optimism for Gen Z. And as easy as it would be to blame "those darn kids," can't we all relate to this? The move to moral relativism didn't happen in a vacuum. There are certainly differences between what various generations think, feel, and believe, but as the social media tower of babble reaches higher and higher, we find ourselves more connected, more exposed to the thoughts and feelings of others, and more susceptible to the cultural patterns that would seek to unite us in our common tendencies.

So what do you get when people have traded truth for relativism, are traumatized and tired, and are looking for ways to improve their mental health? You have an industry ripe to sell a whole heap of materials to help them find everything they need deep inside their own hearts.

Okay. Time to rip off the Band-Aid. Reader, I'm here to tell you: You are not enough.

# 4

# POPSICLES

"Come, Mr. Frodo!" he cried. "I can't carry it for you, but I can carry you."

J. R. R. Tolkien, *The Return of the King*

The mall is an idyllic place when you're a new mom with a two-month-old. Once on a trip to my local galleria, I joyfully sat down on a bench to gaze into my baby's face and give her a chance to look around at all the sensory stimuli waiting to transform her into a little Einstein.

Just kidding. I sat down because I could not walk one more step without fainting from exhaustion in the orthotic shoes I was wearing to help redistribute some of the excess weight that was now crushing my foot bones with every stride. I also stopped because my wee one was not enjoying this little shopping adventure. She'd been wailing ever since I dared to strap her into the car seat to drive there. My free-spirited offspring did not appreciate being constrained by seat belts, strollers, bouncy chairs, swings, or really anything other than my actual arms.

I looked down at the only top I'd been able to squeeze into, my husband's faded extra-large T-shirt, and wondered how on earth I'd managed to gain eighty pounds in pregnancy. I mean . . . I didn't really wonder. I knew it was the cheese. And the donuts. And the ice cream. And the bread and butter. And the meals big enough to feed a group of linebackers. I had just assumed that the weight would magically fall off when the baby was born. I pictured myself being one of those cute moms who strap their little ones to their chests with organic baby wraps as they work out at the gym and run errands. But then my baby was born. Of course, she didn't weigh eighty pounds, so I was stuck with the consequences of nine months' worth of extra helpings of mashed potatoes.

I looked up at some ladies sauntering out of a trendy clothing store. They had perfectly coiffed hair and looked like they'd just come from filming a YouTube makeup tutorial. My mind exploded with confused thoughts as my anxiety grew. *I just want to feel normal. I'm barely hanging on. Will I ever wear regular clothes again? Will my baby ever stop crying?*

Don't get me wrong. I wouldn't trade the first two months of my daughter's life for anything. They were magical in all the right ways, but at the same time, I had spent thirty-three years having to take care of only myself. If I needed a break, I could take one. A snack? I could have one. A nap? I could enjoy one. If I needed to sleep in, go shopping, pay bills, go on a walk, exercise, watch a movie, go to lunch with a friend, or take up a new hobby, I could do so with nothing more than a bit of calendar planning (which I also had plenty of time to do). For the first time, I was forced to realize how selfish and self-focused my entire life had been. I was now, 24-7, at the mercy of the needs of this tiny new human, and I was absolutely exhausted.

Years later, I came across an article addressed to "every exhausted mom out there." It grabbed my attention because it detailed perfectly what I had experienced as a first-time mom. It described a mama hiding in her bathroom to grab just a moment of peace and secretly cry. (I wasn't the only one who did that?) It recounted a mom losing her temper and feeling like the biggest jerk in the world. (Also guilty.) There were descriptions of a mom feeling alone, stuffing her face with food, ordering pizza because she was too tired to cook, and experiencing a big, fat fail when she tried to put her old jeans on. (Yep, yep, check, and yep.) And then there was the big reveal. The answer to all these problems. The sentiment that would turn the whole thing around and give every mom out there some real encouragement. Are you ready for it? The life-changing punch line was this: *You are enough*.

*That's it? That's the big news?* I giggled to myself as I thought about how flat this article would have fallen had I read it in the throes of new motherhood. It didn't help that the ginormous ad to the right of the article featured a photo of a bikini-clad Brazilian supermodel. I mean . . . nothing will make a brand-new mother feel better about herself than being visually accosted by a half-naked seventeen-year-old with no stretch marks or saggy belly skin. But seriously, I am enough? On its face, that is not a message of freedom. It's a message of bondage. "You are enough" is a message that enslaves people to the false idea that they are responsible to be the mastermind of their current circumstances and future realities—even when they feel overwhelmed. It burdens them with the obligation of being the source of their own joy, contentment, and peace. That statement made me think of an earlier era when I thought I was in control of my time, my schedule, and my destiny. All *that* did was make me selfish, self-reliant, and self-focused.

Don't get me wrong. There is great value in reminding women that God has hardwired them with intuitive insights, nurturing qualities, and natural mothering instincts. A woman's body is beautifully designed by God to carry a baby, birth a baby, and feed a baby. In the same way, he has hardwired men in specific ways that make them naturally protective and bent toward working and providing. God creates everyone with certain talents, personalities, and strengths that equip them to fulfill a very specific purpose. (We'll talk more about this in chapter 12.) But that doesn't mean that every person is enough for themselves.

Becoming a mother smacked me in the face with the realization that I am not enough at the deepest level. I never have been. It challenged all my notions of perfection. It removed any illusions that I could somehow draw deep upon the well of my own goodness and give my daughter everything she needed. I couldn't and still can't because I'm not enough. I realized early on that even if I were the best mom who ever lived, I would still get a lot of things wrong. I would miss opportunities and blow it in the parenting department more often than I'd like to admit.

But this is why realizing I am not enough is *actually the best news ever*. You see, Jesus *is* enough, and that's enough for me. We'll get to that in a moment, but for now, hold on to your hat because it's going to get a bit bumpy on our way to freedom.

## WHY DOES THIS SOUND SO GOOD?

The book *Self-Help* was first published (and the term coined) in 1859 by author Samuel Smiles, a dapper Scotsman who sported muttonchops, and it quickly became a bestseller. This is probably because it was about everyone's favorite subject: ourselves. In fact, self-help has become one of the bestselling book genres, and the self-help industry is a billion-dollar enterprise with no signs of slowing down.[1] On the heels of the self-esteem movement that gained major traction through Christian media outlets in the middle of the twentieth century,[2] we have been conditioned to think that if we just love ourselves more, everything will get better.

This is because "you are enough" is based on the assumption that people are basically *good*. Think about it. If that were true, all we would need is to do a deep dive into our own hearts and souls and tap into all the virtue just waiting to be discovered. We could pull from our unlimited reservoir of creativity, power, beauty, truth, and goodness. If that were true, we *would* be enough. If someone is truly struggling with their identity, worth, and even mental health, doesn't it make sense to point out how wonderful they are? And who doesn't want to believe they are inherently good? According to recent research, 81 percent of two thousand Americans surveyed believe just that.[3]

It all sounds so positive and affirming, but deep down we know that humans aren't basically good. Every parent knows this. For example, as soon as children learn to speak, they inherently know how to lie. They know how to be selfish, to cheat, to steal, and to hit. It comes naturally to them. You actually have to teach them to not lie, not put themselves first, not cheat, not take other people's stuff, and not resolve their problems with violence. If you think I'm making this up, test this idea out by giving your only child a little brother or sister and it will be on full display. Am I the only parent whose children are 100 percent disinterested in a particular toy *until* the other sibling wants to play with it? All of a sudden it becomes the most important possession they have ever owned and contains the power to ignite a household war.

## THE BAD PART

The self-esteem and self-help movement can't explain this, but the Bible can. It's a principle theologians call human depravity, and it basically means that people are naturally hardwired to want to get their own way, serve their own desires, and resist letting God be in charge of their lives. But it wasn't always this way. To understand human depravity, we have to understand humans' original purpose. And to understand our purpose, let's talk about Popsicles.

# POPSICLES

When I was a kid, my mom had one of those plastic molds for making homemade Popsicles. It consisted of six hollow rectangle cups that each housed a removable handle that looked like a little sword. The design was perfectly fashioned to let you freeze whatever sweet liquid you poured inside and then slide it out with ease by grasping the lid/handle/sword thingy. My mom was a strict health-food fanatic, so our Popsicles were usually made of unsweetened orange juice or milk mixed with honey. While the neighbor kids always had those cheap store-bought Popsicles that were full of white sugar, delicious chemicals, and red dye, I would grab my bland handcrafted juice pop and head outside to play in the dry California summer heat. The juice and milk pops weren't that bad, but I'd be lying if I said I didn't spend many a lazy summer day gazing longingly at my friends' Big Sticks, Push-Ups, and Rocket Pops.

One blazing day in July, I decided to make my own batch of Popsicles. I poured milk and orange juice into the molds because I had the brilliant idea to make "orangesicles," not realizing you had to sweeten the milk. I opened the drawer where I expected the lid/handle/sword thingies to be, but they weren't there. I searched through every drawer and cabinet in the kitchen but couldn't find them anywhere. (When you have four kids in the same house, getting everyone to return their Popsicle stick to its rightful plastic home would be considered a bona fide miracle.) So I had to get creative. I pulled six teaspoons out of the silverware drawer and plunked one into each of the molds containing the creamy mixture. I stuck them in the freezer and waited for them to solidify.

After a few hours, I pulled them out, grabbed the business end of one of the spoons, and yanked. The spoon slid out clean with no Popsicle attached. *Sigh.* I put them back in the freezer to harden a bit more before I tried the next one. This time, I worked a bit more gingerly. I carefully jiggled it out of its casing and, voilà, a flavorless orangesicle frozen onto a spoon was in my grasp.

As I began to graze on my creation, I encountered some difficulty. First of all, the handle was too short because the top of the spoon had sunk to the bottom of the mold before the mixture froze, leaving nothing but a tiny nub to hold on to. Because of this, the melting Popsicle quickly began dripping onto my fingers and down my hands. There had been nothing to stabilize the spoon in the middle of the mold, so it froze at a lopsided angle. As I ate from the top down, I found it challenging to keep it even on both sides, and eventually half the Popsicle fell off the spoon. The rest quickly dropped as well. The moral of the story? Spoons are fantastic if you need to scoop up food and put it in your mouth. That's their purpose. But they make terrible Popsicle sticks.

Likewise, humans were created in a certain way for a certain purpose. When we try going about life in a way that doesn't align with our purpose, we are like that spoon masquerading as a Popsicle stick, and things will never really work right. Sure, we might manage to stay alive, do some good things in the world, and even find love and some measure of happiness. But we won't hit the mark of what really makes us tick . . . what will satisfy us and make us whole.

Genesis 1:26 gives us a clue to our ultimate purpose.

"God said, 'Let us make man in our image, after our likeness.'" Right from the start, we see that humans were created differently from plants, animals, rocks, and water. Unlike those other creations, we were made in the image and likeness of God himself. This means that every single person who has ever lived has a certain dignity, worth, and value. *But* (yes, there is a big "but") when Adam and Eve decided to turn away from God and pursue their own desires by eating from the tree of the knowledge of good and evil, they unleashed evil—in other words, *sin*—into the world. Then they had children. Their children had children. Just like Adam and Eve were made in the image of God, their children were made in the image of Adam and Eve. Therefore, the image of God was not lost. It was passed down, but it was disfigured. This sin nature was passed down to their descendants.

To put this in Popsicle language, living out our original purpose is like trying to use a Popsicle stick lid/handle/sword thingy that's been warped in the heat of the dishwasher. We've got the right utensil for the right job, and the image of what it was made for still remains. But it has lost its perfect shape, and therefore its ability to fulfill its true purpose. You can try to jam the deformed sword thingy into the plastic mold while repeating the mantra, "You are enough!" But at the end of the day, it will simply not work right. That's because its image has been corrupted, and until it is somehow straightened again, it won't be able to serve as intended as a Popsicle stick.

## THE WARPED PART

Scripture doesn't mince words when it comes to our true condition. The apostle Paul writes in Romans 5:12 that sin and human death came into the world through one man, Adam. Because of this, "death spread to all men because all sinned." Genesis 8:21 tells us that "the intention of man's heart is evil from his youth." Psalm 14:2-3 says that God looks down from heaven to see if there is anyone who does good, but he doesn't find even one. We learn from Jeremiah 17:9 that our hearts are "desperately sick" and deceitful. Ecclesiastes 9:3 depicts the hearts of men as being full of evil and insanity. This means that every single person who has ever lived has distorted the image of God they've been stamped with. That's a hard truth. (It's the "you're not enough" part.)

### Let's compare

Okay. Let's pause for a second. I know this is depressing, but I promise we will get to the good part soon. But first compare the biblical statements above with quotes from some recent books published by self-professed Christians:

> I am exactly enough.[4]

> You deserve goodness.[5]

> I studied the gospel and finally grasped the divine knowledge that I am loved and worthy and enough . . . as I am.[6]

When it comes to human nature, do you see the difference between the grim picture the Bible paints versus the over-the-top optimistic one painted by some modern writers? It's not just a little bit different. It's the exact opposite. Thankfully, the Bible can also explain why this is the case. In fact, the entire first chapter of Romans is dedicated to demonstrating this phenomenon. Do you want to know the origin story of literally every false religion, errant philosophy, and mistaken ideology?

God spoke through the apostle Paul to give us a clue. In verse 19, he explains that everyone who has ever lived can look out into the world and know that God exists. But it doesn't stop there. We can actually learn certain characteristics about him and how he works in the world. That's right. No one who has ever been born is without access to knowledge about God, even if they've never heard of the Bible. In fact, Paul says that this revelation is actually quite plain. It's perfectly clear. In verse 20, he writes, "His invisible attributes, namely, his eternal power and divine nature, have been clearly perceived, ever since the creation of the world, in the things that have been made." Paul goes on to explain that this is why no human can make any excuses when it comes to rejecting God.

Psalm 19 illustrates this point beautifully: "The heavens declare the glory of God, and the sky above proclaims his handiwork. Day to day pours out speech, and night to night reveals knowledge" (verses 1-2). Paul starts with the fact that people already know God. So when they choose to turn away from him, it's because they refuse to honor him as God. He then gives them what they want: He allows them to worship the creation rather than the creator. Very often, they just turn inward and worship themselves. That's every false religion in a nutshell.

But this is not without consequences. This stirs the Lord's anger toward them because they aren't doing this in ignorance. They are willingly and knowingly pushing truth down to chase after lies. Perhaps this is why the apostle Paul breaks it down the way he does in Ephesians 2:1-3:

> You were dead in the trespasses and sins in which you once walked, following the course of this world, following the prince of the power of the air, the spirit that is now at work in the sons of disobedience— among whom we all once lived in the passions of our flesh, carrying out the desires of the body and the mind, and were by nature children of wrath, like the rest of mankind.

Wow. What a difference. Culture says you and I should think, *I am enough.* The Bible says that by nature, I am a "child of wrath."

## THE GOOD PART

Okay, I promised we would get to the good part, and here we are. Paul has told us that, by nature, we are not even close to enough (children of wrath, anyone?). But he delivers good news in 2 Corinthians 5:21, where he says that even though Jesus "knew no sin," he was made to be sin (by his death on the cross) so that "we might become the righteousness of

God." In other words, Jesus covered our not-enough-ness with his enough-ness to make us *enough* before God. That's right: *Jesus is enough*, and when we put our faith and trust in him, we find peace with God.

You don't have to be enough because Jesus already is. He explains this quite plainly in John 15 when he compares himself to a vine. Those who believe in him are like branches growing from and dependent upon that vine. Jesus tells us that when we abide in him and he abides in us, we will bear good fruit. In nature, a branch that is cut off from its vine will quickly die. It will never bear fruit in and of itself. It is not enough. It's the same with us humans. Jesus tells us why this is the case: "For apart from me you can do nothing" (verse 5).

Remember Psalm 14, which describes God looking down from heaven and finding not even one good person? In Romans 3:10-12, Paul quotes that psalm and, several verses later, says that everyone is guilty: "All have sinned and fall short of the glory of God" (verse 23). But not long after, Paul comes galloping into the story with the really good news. Romans 5:1 tells us, "Since we have been justified by faith, we have peace with God through our Lord Jesus Christ." Whether we win or lose, find happiness or suffering in this life, crush our career goals or wind up homeless, we can achieve the purpose for which we were created: finding peace with God, worshiping him, and enjoying him forever. You will never be good enough, smart enough, ambitious enough, athletic enough, disciplined enough, strong enough, gracious enough, loving enough, honest enough, gifted enough, tough enough, gentle enough, talented enough, or dedicated enough. *You. Are. Not. Enough.* This news humbles the mighty and elevates the humble. That's the beautiful paradox of the gospel: that "while we were still sinners, Christ died for us" (Romans 5:8).

You are not enough, but when your trust is placed in Jesus, his enough-ness is transferred to you. Isn't that good news? If you agree, I've got some more for you. Armed with the knowledge that you are not enough in and of yourself, you can be in a better position to prioritize who comes first in your life.

Hint: #Iamsecond.

# 5

# ARMAGEDDON

## You Should Put Yourself First

No one is useless in this world who
lightens the burdens of another.

Charles Dickens, *Doctor Marigold*

Every summer has its blockbuster movies, and 1998 was no
exception. Crowds flocked to the theaters to watch Bruce
Willis save the world from being obliterated by an asteroid in
the much-anticipated release *Armageddon*. That was a pressure cooker of a year, with the president embroiled in scan-
dal ("I did not have sexual relations with that woman!"), an
uptick in abortion clinic bombings, and the looming threat
of Iraq refusing to get rid of its weapons of mass destruction.
There were school shootings, Saddam Hussein was wreaking
havoc, and Pakistan was testing nuclear bombs. It was all very
intense, and the American public was ripe for a diversion.

I grabbed my popcorn and soda and found a seat in the
middle of the row all by myself. I've always considered it a

special treat to go to a movie alone. No interruptions. No chitchat. I had just endured a particularly tough couple of years, so I was also ready to be distracted by space rocks, astronauts, and nuclear solutions. What better way to entertain a stressed-out population than for Charlton Heston to soberly describe an asteroid impact that took place millions of years ago, wiping out the dinosaurs and nearly all life on earth. The movie opens with syncopated strings accenting pulsing snare drums and cymbals as a super serious Heston warns, "It happened before . . . it *will* happen again." (Cue more scary music.) "It's just a question of *when*."

Turns out, Heston was correct. NASA spots an asteroid the size of Texas hurtling toward Earth. It is due to make impact in just eighteen days. If this cosmic torpedo strikes the planet, it's game over. The literal end of the world. Government eggheads and NASA scientists jump in the think tank to come up with a master plan to save the world from impending doom. They decide the best course of action is to drill a hole in the asteroid, pack it with a nuclear bomb, and blow it up before it breaches the earth's atmosphere. This is a job for no mere astronaut. Enter Harry Stamper, the world's best deep-core oil driller. NASA convinces this grumpy yet good-hearted antihero to fly to space and do what only he can—commandeer a humongous rig called the *Armadillo*, drill to the core of the asteroid, and detonate a nuclear bomb. This should split the asteroid in two, causing it to miss the earth by hundreds of miles. Harry recruits his most trusted workers, a scrappy band of misfits who must quickly learn how to be astronauts before blasting off in T-minus twelve days. The training scenes are set to Aerosmith's "Sweet Emotion" and it's all just so 1990s. (For the record, I'm here for it.)

A consistent theme that drives Harry's character throughout the film is the loving yet turbulent relationship he has with his twentysomething daughter, Grace, played by Liv Tyler. Plot twist—Grace is in love with A.J. (Ben Affleck), one of Harry's best employees, who is very talented but a bit of a hotshot. When Harry discovers this, his helicopter parenting skills kick into high gear and he forbids the relationship, taking Grace with him to NASA headquarters to get her away from A.J. (Memo to parents: Want to fan the flames of love between your daughter and that outlaw boyfriend you hate? Ban them from seeing each other. I mean . . . did Harry even read *Romeo and Juliet?*) But darn it, A.J. is his best worker, so Harry has to swallow his pride and take him along. In the meantime, A.J. proposes to Grace, which is met with Harry's not so subtle disapproval.

Tension mounts as the impact event looms, and Harry and his rowdy crew blast off to save the world. Just about everything that could go wrong does. The space station they stop to refuel at explodes, their thrusters are hit with debris, a bunch of people die, and they are forced to crash-land on the asteroid. They touch down on a section that is made of hardened iron, which destroys their first drill head and blows their transmission. They lose contact with Earth, more people die, and it all feels pretty bleak at this point. After a real nail-biter of a time, they end up drilling the hole and successfully inserting the bomb. But Houston, we have a problem. With only eighteen minutes left, they realize someone must stay behind to trigger the bomb manually, effectively giving their life to save the world. But who will it be? They draw straws, and A.J. is chosen. Harry helps A.J. travel down to the core of the asteroid, and at the last minute, takes A.J.'s place on the suicide mission. A.J., along with the remaining survivors, travels safely home. Once back on Earth, A.J. and Grace get married in a melodramatic sequence so hokey it is rivaled only by 1991's *Robin Hood: Prince of Thieves*, in which Kevin Costner as Robin Hood informs Maid Marian (in the worst English accent ever), "I would die fer yew." (Score another one for the nineties.)

Harry Stamper, our cranky protagonist and unlikely hero, gives his life to save the world. Now *that's* a good story. It's also a story that is retold over and over. From Gandalf to Ironman, every time a person gives his life for others, he is hailed as a hero. That's what heroes do. Jesus articulated it this way: "Greater love has no one than this, that someone lay down his life for his friends" (John 15:13).

Now let's rewind and imagine that, just prior to hearing from NASA, Harry Stamper had read a bestselling self-help book encouraging him to make himself his top priority. Fueled up on positive self-affirmations and self-love mantras, and armed with a printed goal sheet, Harry decides at the last minute that his unfulfilled dreams demand more time. After all, what kind of an example will he be setting for his daughter if he gives up on his deepest ambitions now? What message will that send to her about *her* undeveloped aspirations? He lets A.J. take the fall for humanity, zooms back to Earth, and invests in that start-up company he's always thought would change the world. Good job, Harry.

Well, that would be a terrible movie. I imagine people would be demanding their money back after that box-office failure. Why? Because our hero would really just be a selfish coward; deep down, we all know that putting others first is more noble than being selfish. We know that prioritizing our own dreams, ambitions, and goals over the needs of others is downright evil . . . in fact, it's contemptible.

## WHY DOES THIS SOUND SO GOOD?

Back before Netflix existed and binge-watching was a thing, people actually had to wait until a certain night of the week to watch their favorite show. When I was a little girl, my mom would make popcorn and hot cocoa for the week's installment of the popular show *The A-Team*, which featured four ex-soldiers who fled to Los Angeles after being convicted of a crime they didn't commit. They got into all kinds of trouble, which often included a shower of bullets propelled from machine guns, but no one ever got hurt. We didn't question it, and it was magical.

Every once in a while, my favorite commercial about Calgon bath powder would interrupt the A-Team's shenanigans. The ad highlighted a thirtysomething working mom who was absolutely exasperated by all her responsibilities. The dog! The job! The kids! Oh, it was just all too much, and she would eventually demand, "Calgon, take me away!" Instantly the screen would flash to her tired body immersed in bubbles and relaxing in a colossal round bathtub that was apparently located somewhere in ancient Greece. With the columns of the Parthenon surrounding her cauldron of pleasure, this exhausted mom soaked away every one of her troubles, thanks to this enchanted Calgon product. Every time I saw the ad, I was like—*Note to self: Buy Mom some Calgon because she deserves to bathe with the people from Olympia.* She had four kids in school, sports, and music lessons, and my dad traveled for a living. It was the least I could do.

Putting yourself first sounds good because we all know that an exhausted, angry, and overworked person is no good for anyone. Blocking it all out and jumping into a warm, effervescent basin of luxury sounds like just the thing to reset our patience and wash our worries away. And please. Moms. Listen to me. If you are at the end of your rope, go take a bath. Parents, get in a workout, go out to lunch, chop wood, or watch your favorite sports team. Do whatever it is that recharges and energizes you to better serve your family. It's important that we take care of our minds and bodies as good stewards of the gift of life God has given us. But if our understanding of ourselves isn't rooted in Scripture, it can become easy to confuse taking care of ourselves with the world's idea of "self-care."

## SISTERS ARE DOIN' IT FOR THEMSELVES

Remember those eighty pounds I gained in pregnancy? Several months after my daughter was born, I became increasingly anxious about how miserable I looked and felt. I was also in the middle of a faith crisis (see my book *Another Gospel?* for details of that journey), and life seemed to be spinning out of control. I told myself I wanted to get healthy and strong for my daughter, but I was overwhelmed with self-loathing and disgust over my weight. It was all about me.

I fell back into familiar and sinful patterns from my past. I lost the weight. And then some. I was not healthy. But here's the thing: Losing the weight didn't make the self-loathing go away. It only continued to grow worse. What began as an attempt to "get healthy for my daughter" spiraled into a deadly and cyclical pattern that drained me of energy and flung me into a constant state of shame and bondage. When I felt the guilt and self-hatred surrounding my body, I went inward. I sought to control the situation and fix it myself. I didn't pray about it. I didn't ask God to help me. In fact, at the time, I wasn't even sure God existed. I felt fat and alone, and I attempted to pull myself up by my bootstraps. But pulling yourself up by your bootstraps is physically impossible. Think about it. Seriously, try it. It's literally not possible.

In her wonderful book, *You're Not Enough and That's Okay*, Allie Beth Stuckey makes sense of what was going on inside me: "The self can't be both the problem and the solution. If our problem is that we're insecure or unfulfilled, we're not going to be able to find the antidote to these things in the same place our insecurities and fear are coming from."[1] I hated myself for my unhealthy patterns, and at the same time, I thought I could fix myself. But it just doesn't work that way.

Shortly after I lost the weight, I got pregnant again and gained seventy pounds. But this time, my relationship with God had mended a bit. I promised him and myself that even if I had to live the rest of my life heavier than I wanted to be, I would surrender my weight to God and trust him. I confessed what was going on to my husband and asked him to help keep the light on it by asking me how I was doing with food. I vowed to be honest and I always was—even when the answer was painful and embarrassing. Slowly I began to heal and recover. To this day Mike still asks me how I'm doing with food, and I just love him for it.

Years later, after my faith had been reconstructed, I needed to have a headshot photo taken for an apologetics blog I was starting up. I did not lose weight for that. For some reason I did make the brilliant decision to cut my hair short and wear it naturally curly, and I don't have an excuse for that. (Insert sarcasm here.) Along with my bad hair choice, my weight stayed the same for over seven years. In other words, I didn't put my own desires, ambitions, and vanity before my husband and kids, who needed a healthy wife and mom. In fact, refusing to lose weight was exactly how I put others first . . . for a while. But as time went on, that decision morphed into an excuse to overeat and be lazy and inactive. I packed on even more weight, which made it difficult to get out of bed in the morning. I became winded doing simple tasks and found myself looking for excuses not to play with my kids.

One Christmas Eve as I shoveled custard filling into my face with a giant wooden spoon, wondering how much I could skim off the top and still have enough left over for the pie I was baking, I had an epiphany. *Something has got to change. I can't live like this any longer.* I realized that in my attempt to course correct my eating disorder, I went from one extreme to another. I had created an imbalance by trading extreme measures to stay thin with extreme indulgence. None of this was in the best interest of my family. I chose selfishness the first time (I wanted to be skinny more than I wanted to give my kids a *healthy* mom), and I was choosing selfishness again (I wanted to overeat and be inactive more than I wanted to give my kids an *active* mom).

Every time we choose to put our own wants and desires before the needs of others, it creates an imbalance. This time, I wanted to get in shape for my kids, so I asked for help, followed a plan, and chose to not indulge my every craving. God also gave me the beautiful gift of running and hiking, but that's another story for another time. Slowly but surely, some of the weight began to come off, and it no longer hurt to walk from my bed to the bathroom in the morning. I felt so much better now that I had put the needs of others before my own needs. I'm still working through it, and I'd be kidding myself if I said I've got it all figured out. But I know that when I go for a run, lift weights, and eat reasonable portions of healthy food, I am a much better mom and wife. I have energy to write all day while my kids are at school and then be totally present and engaged with them when they get home. I am thankful to God for that gift. But it wouldn't have happened had I continued to choose myself first.

## WWJD?

The Bible has quite a bit to say on the topic of putting others first, and much of it comes directly from the lips of Jesus himself. When he walked the earth, he was regularly opposed by two groups of religious leaders, the Pharisees and the Sadducees. The Pharisees were very strict legalists when it came to the law. They added a whole bunch of oral rules and traditions to the law to try to keep themselves distinct from culture and pure before God. The Sadducees, on the other hand, rejected these oral traditions and denied the Resurrection. But despite this clash of opinions, one thing united them: They both hated Jesus big-time. Both groups constantly tried to trip him up, entrap him, and prove him wrong.

One day, when the Pharisees heard that Jesus had dodged the Sadducees' intellectual bullets like Neo from *The Matrix*, they chose one of their legal experts to test him. In Matthew 22:36, this lawyer asked him which was the greatest commandment from the law. (With hundreds of laws to choose from, I'm sure he thought he had Jesus stumped with that one!) Without missing a beat, Jesus quoted two verses from the Scriptures. First, he cited a famous passage from Deuteronomy 6:5, which the Jews call the Shema: "You shall love the LORD your God with all your heart and with all your soul and with all your might." Next, he quoted Leviticus 19:18: "You shall love your neighbor as yourself." Jesus wrapped up this exchange with a bold claim in verse 40: "On these two commandments depend all the Law and the

Prophets." (In first-century Jewish culture, "the Law and the Prophets" was a reference to the entire Old Testament.)

Stop and think for a moment how savagely brilliant this was. Literally every moral command in the Old Testament law will be followed perfectly if you obey those two commands. Take, for example, the Ten Commandments. The first one says, "You shall have no other gods before me" (Exodus 20:3). If you love God with all your heart, you won't put any gods before him. The second commandment is similar, as it basically says that making carved images to worship is a no-no. Once again, if you love God with all that you are, you won't do that. Taking the name of the Lord in vain? You're good to go if you love God first. The fourth through tenth commandments prohibit things like adultery, murder, stealing, lying, and coveting. Think about it. If you love your neighbor as yourself, *you won't do those things to your neighbors.* Brilliant!

Some interpreters have taken the passage "Love your neighbor as yourself" as a mandate for loving yourself. But as one commentator writes, "In our narcissistic culture, inundated as we are with psychology, most have taken this as a command for self-love. . . . The text, however, does not command self-love; possibly it recognizes its existence, at the very most it legitimates it. . . . Certainly 'as yourself' does not include the command to love oneself or state that one should love oneself."[2] Notice that Jesus doesn't have to command you to love yourself. He assumes you already know how to do that. He actually has to tell you to put God first and others second because this does not come naturally. The apostle Paul summed it up like this: "No one ever hated his own flesh, but nourishes and cherishes it, just as Christ does the church" (Ephesians 5:29). What does come naturally to human beings, however, is sin. It's all over Jesus' teachings. Take a look.

Jesus famously said, "Do to others as you would have them do to you" (Luke 6:31, NIV). Now many a skeptic has charged Jesus with ripping off older wisdom here since similar versions of this command are found in the sayings of teachers who came before Jesus, like Confucius and Buddha, as well as in Hinduism and Greek philosophy.[3] (Then again, Leviticus 19:18 basically says the same thing and was written long before these other guys lived.) But here's what the skeptics miss. In every one of the examples above, the Golden Rule is in the negative form—something like "Do *not* do to others what you *don't* want them to do to you." But that is not so difficult, is it? When worded this way, you don't actually have to *do anything*. You can be indifferent. You can still put yourself first and simply avoid being a huge jerk to someone else. But that isn't good enough for Jesus. In typical fashion, he flips the idea on its head and turns a don't into a do. (Remember the Sermon on the Mount, in which Jesus said it's not enough simply to abstain from physically committing adultery, but if you lust after someone in your heart, you're already guilty of adultery? It's like that.) In other words, Jesus won't allow you and me to skate by. It is impossible to obey the Golden Rule and put yourself first at the same time. According to Jesus, you have to think of what you would do if you put yourself first and go *do that* to someone else.

But that's not all Jesus had to say on the subject: He once sat his disciples down and told them, "If anyone would be first, he must be last of all and servant of all" (Mark 9:35). Knowing that people will get all worked up about their clothes, what they will eat, and how their lives will ultimately end up, he said, "Do not be anxious about your life" (Matthew 6:25). After pointing out how God demonstrates his faithfulness to meet their physical needs, he instructed: "Seek first the kingdom of God and his righteousness, and all these things will be added to you" (verse 33). Then in Matthew 10, he offered a hard truth. If anyone won't take up their cross—an instrument of death—and follow him, that person is not worthy of him (verse 38). He continued: "Whoever finds his life will lose it, and whoever loses his life for my sake will find it" (verse 39). In Matthew 5:39-41, he shocked his followers by telling them that if someone slapped them on one check, they should offer them the other one. If someone sued them for one shirt, they should give them their coat too. If someone forced them to walk one mile with them, they should make it two. He continued, "Give to the one who begs from you, and do not refuse the one who would borrow from you" (Matthew 5:42).

These passages do not exactly describe the poster child of self-empowerment. Jesus couldn't be any clearer about what our first priority should be. Not ourselves—but God, his kingdom, his righteousness, and other people. Building on what he had commanded his followers in Matthew 10:38, he stated even more plainly what it takes to call yourself a Jesus follower: "If anyone would come after me, let him deny himself and take up his cross and follow me" (Matthew 16:24).

Jesus modeled this self-denial in his own life. In fact, he described his purpose for coming to earth in Mark 10:45, NIV: "The Son of Man did not come to be served, but to serve, and to give his life as a ransom for many." Remember when he said that loving your neighbor as yourself was the second greatest commandment? He tied it together here by describing what that type of love looks like. He gave his life for us. He lived this teaching to the fullest, sealing it with his own blood.

The apostle Paul recognized this about Jesus. In Philippians 2:6-8, Paul pointed out that Jesus, who was in the form of God, decided to give up his divine privileges, taking the form of a servant . . . a human. Then "he humbled himself by becoming obedient to the point of death, even death on a cross" (verse 8). Throughout his letters, Paul tells us how we should model Christ in the way we treat others. If there is any question as to whether or not Paul thinks you should put yourself first, consider this striking declaration: "For those who are self-seeking and do not obey the truth, but obey unrighteousness, there will be wrath and fury" (Romans 2:8).

It's vital that we keep our life, loves, and actions properly ordered, with God first and others second. This keeps us from an endless pendulum swing between extremes like idleness and overwork, self-hatred and self-obsession. This is not only wise, but it also brings a reward: "Whoever refreshes others will be refreshed" (Proverbs 11:25, NIV). See how that works?

It might feel overwhelming when we think about how hard it is to actually live this out, but think of it this way: When we dedicate our lives to serving God and others, we are not like a car running out of gas. We are more like a house with solar panels. Those panels face the sun and convert sunlight into energy, which in turn powers the house. It's a continual process of giving and renewal.[4]

### HOW TO BE YOUR "AUTHENTIC" SELF

| <u>Cultural</u> | <u>Countercultural</u> |
| --- | --- |
| Put yourself first. | Put up with the failings of others (Romans 15:1). |
| Outdo yourself in work or leisure—whatever it takes to make your dreams come true. | Outdo one another in showing honor (Romans 12:10). |
| Seek good for yourself. | Seek the good of others (1 Corinthians 10:24). |
| Count your "likes" and accomplishments. | Count others as more significant than you (Philippians 2:3). |
| Exalt yourself so you can be number one. | Crucify yourself so Christ can live in you (Galatians 2:20). |

## LET'S COMPARE

While the biblical call to put ourselves at least third is fresh in our minds, ponder these quotes from popular "Christian" books:

You are meant to be the hero of your own story.[5]

I am willing to be the villain in someone else's story if it means I can be the hero of my own.[6]

We do not need more selfless women. What we need right now is more women who have detoxed themselves so completely from the world's expectations that they are full of nothing but themselves. What we need are women who are *full of themselves*. A woman who is full of herself knows and trusts herself enough to say and do what must be done. She lets the rest burn.[7]

You should be the very first of your priorities![8]

I'll abandon everyone else's expectations of me before I'll abandon myself. I'll disappoint everyone else before I'll disappoint myself. I'll forsake all others before I'll forsake myself. Me and myself: *We are till death do us part.*[9]

What a difference. In Glennon Doyle's smash-hit book *Untamed,* the former Christian mommy blogger turned best-selling author and national speaker recounts the decision she made to leave her husband for the woman she fell in love with at first sight. Comparing herself to a caged cheetah she saw at a local zoo, she decided to break out of her own domesticated prison and argues that putting her romantic needs first is what actually makes her a good mother. Crediting Swiss psychiatrist Carl Jung for getting to the heart of the matter, she writes:

Mothers have martyred themselves in their children's names since the beginning of time. We have lived as if she who disappears the most, loves the most. We have been conditioned to prove our love by slowly ceasing to exist.

What a terrible burden for children to bear—to know that they are the reason their mother stopped living. What a terrible burden for our daughters to bear—to know that if they choose to become mothers, this will be their fate, too. . . .

Jung suggested: *There is no greater burden on a child than the unlived life of a parent.* . . .

I would never again settle for a relationship or life less beautiful than the one I'd want for my child.

I'd divorce Craig. Because I am a mother. And I have responsibilities.[10]

Compare her story to Elisabeth Elliot, whose husband was famously killed by the Waorani people in Ecuador after attempting to bring the gospel to their remote tribe. This untamed beast of a woman went back to the very people who had killed her beloved Jim and preached the gospel to them, three-year-old daughter in tow. (Because she is a mother. And she had responsibilities.) She lived among them, sharing the love of Christ (which, by the way, is not the type of love that tries to prove anything) and leading many to the Lord. After two years of laying down her life for others, she came back to the United States, eventually writing more than twenty books, sharing wisdom from biblical truth and her lifelong dedication to Jesus. She didn't chase her inner cheetah into personal contentment. She practiced self-sacrifice and true biblical devotion.

When Jesus tells us to pick up our crosses and die, he gives us something even better in exchange . . . his very self. This is something self-help culture will never understand. All the self-obsessed books in the world can't fathom that a person could possibly find peace and joy—even in the confines of an unhappy marriage, an unrealized dream, or a life that falls short of their expectation. They don't understand how putting God and others first actually provides a stable platform upon which to stand and weather all manner of storms. This is why their inner cheetahs keep chasing their tails, looking for the next relationship high, career success, or hit of happiness.

Elisabeth Elliot laid hold of a deeper strength. When faced with situations in which she found herself unfulfilled and unhappy, she refused to fade into nothingness. She rejected the urge to defy God's Word or redefine his holiness. She dismissed the idea that she had to stop existing or make her personal happiness her highest priority. She recognized that this is not what Jesus calls us to do when he bids us come and die. She understood that putting God first meant planting her feet firmly on the bedrock of truth. She would not be moved when winds of boredom blew and storms of doubt, dissatisfaction, and suffering raged. That, dear reader, is the opposite of disappearing. How did she do it? She once wrote, "The secret is Christ in me, not me in a different set of circumstances."[11]

With Christ in you, you can walk through anything. You

can be unfulfilled sexually, emotionally, and intellectually, yet still be 100 percent *free* and filled with a deep, abiding joy. It's true! But you can get there only if you start by utterly refusing to put yourself first. You are not even second. You are third. Maybe fourth. You get it.

Now that you've plumbed the depths of your soul only to find a sinner there, the world will tell you that you should air all your dirty laundry like a cheap reality show in the name of authenticity. I'm here to tell you. You've been sold a barrel of baloney. Authenticity is *not* everything.

6

# CHEERLEADER

Authenticity Is Everything

It's a life's work to see yourself for what you really
are and even then you might be wrong. And that
is somethin I don't want to be wrong about.

Cormac McCarthy, *No Country for Old Men*

I knew exactly who I was when I was five years old. From
the second I laid eyes on the blue spring floor, smelled the
chalk clouds clapped from leather handgrips, and ran my
hand across the smooth oak uneven bars, I knew. *I am a gymnast.* I knew without a doubt this was the planet I was from.
These were my people. For the next several years, gymnastics
became my life. It became my identity. I felt like my most
authentic self when I was tumbling on the mat, leaping on
the balance beam, or swinging on the uneven bars. At the
time, I mistakenly thought that what I do is who I am. In
other words, I conflated authenticity with identity.

At one of my first lessons, I observed another gymnast do
a back walkover, which is basically a backward cartwheel. You

raise your arms in the air, bend all the way back until your palms are flat on the ground, and then kick your legs over until they reach the floor and you stand back up. No one told me this was something you had to learn, not something you just get up and do. So I just got up and did it. My coach was stunned and informed my mom that I was a natural gymnast.

After a couple of years, my parents, being the eternally supportive people they are, enrolled me in a different gym across town that had once produced an athlete who went to the Olympic trials. She didn't make the team, but I didn't care because this gym had Olympic dreams and so did I. If you had asked me who I was when I was nine years old, I would have answered without hesitation. "Duh. I am a gymnast who is going to be an Olympic gold medalist like Mary Lou Retton." Turns out, I wasn't as good as I thought I was, but that is beside the point. I wanted to glorify God with my talent, so my big dream was to win Olympic gold and then move to Ethiopia, where I would preach the gospel and teach gymnastics lessons to all the starving children I saw on the television commercials. The obvious next step.

Around that same time, my mom made me take piano lessons, which I absolutely hated. I believed the piano was Satan incarnate, and I daydreamed about plucking out each ivory key with a screwdriver. I loathed those lessons. I resented them. I abhorred them. I detested them. I abominated them. I despised them. (Author's note: Yes, I consulted a thesaurus to properly convey my emotional disposition toward said piano lessons in hopes of making myself clear.) I did not like practicing at all. When I wasn't at school or the gym, I wanted to spend every remaining moment in my backyard cartwheeling across the handmade balance beam my dad had built for me. I most certainly did not want to spend thirty minutes a day trapped in front of an apparatus that can't even figure out if it's a percussion instrument or stringed one. I begged my mom to let me quit. For *years*. Finally, she ended the horrific punishment I had done nothing to deserve and would clearly not need as an Olympic-winning gymnastics missionary philanthropist.

But then something happened. As a successful piano lesson dropout, I realized I no longer *had* to play. So one day, I sat on the piano bench, touched my fingers to the keys, and pressed the notes that came to my heart. And then I started singing. I couldn't believe what was happening. Out of nowhere, I was writing a song about my love for Jesus. And I liked it. I felt the presence of God. It wasn't until years later that I found language to describe what had happened to me. The movie *Chariots of Fire* tells the story of Scottish runner and devout Christian Eric Liddell, who believed that God had called him to race for God's glory. In a famous scene, he says, "I believe that God made me for a purpose. . . . But he also made me fast. And when I run I feel his pleasure."[1] Yes, that was it. I had felt God's pleasure that day when I sang and played piano for his glory. I informed my mom and dad that the gymnastics gig was done and that I was called to be a musician. My parents, still being the eternally supportive people they are, dropped a thirty-day notice on the gym faster than you can say, "Yurchenko double pike." I found out later that two weeks before my big announcement, they had prayed that God would redirect me if gymnastics wasn't his will for my life. I always took that as confirmation I was on the right path.

My dad began teaching me how to use his home studio equipment, and I wrote like the world was running out of songs. I told all my friends I was going to be a Christian recording artist one day and truly believed I would change the world with music. (How's that for plucky optimism?) I had no plan B. By the time I hit high school, I started performing concerts for my youth group and at other small local churches. I also played softball and became a cheerleader to scratch the gymnastics itch that lingered from childhood. But music is what I was made for. I knew . . . *this is who I am. I am a singer-songwriter.*

## BRANDED

Toward the end of our performing career, ZOEgirl was invited to join a national tour that was the "little sister" of an incredibly successful global women's ministry that produced weekend events attended by several million people. Now this organization had funneled all its resources, talent energy, and knowledge into an event aimed at teenage girls.

With big-time sponsors and major Christian corporations behind it, this tour was highly anticipated, well-funded, and heavily controlled. Every song was meticulously chosen, and the staging was painstakingly choreographed. My bandmates and I were informed that every word uttered from the stage would be scripted. We, along with every performer, were assigned a particular image that the girls in attendance could relate to. One was the "bohemian chick." Another was "the sporty one." There was "the edgy one," "the artsy one," and "the funny one." Dang. With bohemian, edgy, and artsy taken, I ended up with the leftover. I would henceforth be known as "the cheerleader." The message was implicit but clear: This is who you are. Stay on script, and don't break character. I was uncomfortable with this arrangement, but when you're in a situation like that, you do everything you can to talk yourself into cooperating. *Maybe I can just say what they want me to say because some young girl will come here and get saved. Maybe this is a lesson in submitting to leadership.* Night after night, "the artsy one" would announce that in high school, she was an artist and a singer. This was always met with boisterous cheers and applause. Then it was time for my big line: "And I was . . . a cheerleader!" It was a setup that was meant to be received negatively. I felt like such an idiot. It wasn't entirely untrue. I *was* a cheerleader in high school. But it was a blip on my radar. It wasn't *who I am*.

When ZOEgirl ended, I was burned-out and restless. At thirty-two, I had never achieved my dream of being a solo artist and singer-songwriter who changed the world for God. I waited so many years, yet it never happened. I had given what I thought were the best years of my life to touring with a girl pop group, something I had never been sure I wanted to do in the first place. Now, it might be tempting to think that performing to more than a million people, selling hundreds of thousands of albums, and seeing your face blown up to the size of a brontosaurus on a billboard would be the quintessential definition of living the dream. But that wasn't *my* dream. It wasn't *who I am*. I wanted to see hundreds, even thousands, of people come to Christ through the deep, impactful lyrics and moving melodies God had put on my heart. Instead, I was actually quite an emotional wreck during those years, and the whole experience is a bit tainted by that. As a side note, I've since shared these thoughts with audiences across the country, and many a ZOEgirl fan has come up to me and reduced me to tears with their encouragement. One young lady told me: "I was one of those little zoegirl fans who came to your concert. I felt so alone as a Christian at my school, and you three inspired and encouraged me to stand strong in my convictions and keep going in my faith. I just want you to know that it was all worth it." And it was worth it. But I couldn't see it at the time.

I had bought into the lie that I was defined by what I did, what I wanted, and what I loved. I must have been harping on this in a particular counseling session because a therapist I began seeing toward the end of ZOEgirl's run (who had the wisdom of Solomon and the patience of Job) looked at me intently and gently asked, "What if you got throat cancer and could never sing again?" I was dumbstruck. She had stumped me. After all, I was made to sing, and if I couldn't sing, who was I? After a long pause, I stuttered, "I–I–I don't know. I don't know." In the moment, the question seemed like an oxymoron. If I lost my voice, I would cease to be *me*. My authentic self would be lost. I've pondered this question for years. The answer is so clear now. But back then, it was like asking me who I would be if I didn't exist.

## ARTIFICIAL AUTHENTICITY VS. BIBLICAL AUTHENTICITY

To get authenticity right, we must define our terms. Because words. *Authenticity* is one of those words that has gotten a modern-day makeover. If you search the internet, you'll find all sorts of working definitions. Here are three:

"Living your life according to your own values and goals."[2]

"Acting in ways that show your true self and how you feel."[3]

"Real or genuine: not copied or false."[4]

Notice how all three are slightly different. The first is built solely upon the foundation of self. I suspect it's what many people mean when they speak of living authentically today. According to that definition, I make the rules and I live by them, no matter what anyone else says. It's another way of saying, "Live your truth." But as we learned in chapter 3, operating by our own truth doesn't work out so well. That's artificial authenticity.

What about the next definition? "Acting in ways that show your true self and how you feel." That gets us a little closer. We *should* be honest about our feelings and celebrate our unique gifts, talents, and personalities. We aren't gingerbread men all cut out of the same mold for the exact same purpose. We shouldn't show up to church and shine on about how victorious our week was if we barely got out of bed that morning.

What about that third one? "Real or genuine: not copied or false." This nails it. This definition includes the idea that we should be honest about our feelings (genuine), but it takes the context out of the realm of *self* and places it in the realm of *truth*. That's the opposite of artificial authenticity, which is an oxymoron. Living according to *the* truth is the most authentic way to live because it's what we were made for.

The Bible has a lot to say about who we are and how to live authentically in that identity. According to John 1:12, everyone who has received Christ and believed in his name has been given the right to become a child of God. It's wonderful and mind-boggling—our identity is no longer bound up in ourselves but in him. The apostle Paul tells us in Galatians 2:20 that when we become followers of Jesus, it's as if we've been crucified right along with Christ. This means that we have effectively died to our old lives and aren't living for ourselves anymore. In fact, Paul writes, "It is no longer I who live, but Christ who lives in me." That doesn't mean the unique talents, personalities, and giftings we've been created with are dead. Rather, we continually put to death the sin that stains and taints those God-given gifts and qualities. This frees us to be who we were truly created to be.

Paul tells us in 2 Corinthians 5:17 that if anyone is in Christ, he is a brand-new creation. Everything in the past is gone, and we are literally made new. What a foundation to build upon! Authenticity begins with a death. Specifically, it's a death to self and a reorientation toward living for Christ.

## FINDING YOUR TRUE AUTHENTIC SELF?

Christ paid an incalculable price to redeem us; it's no wonder we get into trouble when we emphasize our fallen selves above him. Brené Brown is a research professor, speaker, and author who writes about shame and vulnerability. Although baptized into the Episcopal church as a child, she was raised Catholic before she left organized religion as a young adult. After about twenty years, she and her husband returned to the Episcopal church because she wanted to find "a spiritual home where there is room at the table for everyone."[5] She is widely popular in the self-help industry, and many Christians look to her for wisdom on issues related to authenticity. In her book *Braving the Wilderness* she writes:

> True belonging is the spiritual practice of believing in and belonging to yourself so deeply that you can share your most authentic self with the world and find sacredness in both being a part of something and standing alone in the wilderness. True belonging doesn't require you to *change* who you are; it requires you to *be* who you are.[6]

Jen Hatmaker includes Brown's quote in her book *Fierce, Free, and Full of Fire*. In her commentary, she mentions her "pesky prophetic nature," which keeps her from thriving as a "female leader in evangelical subculture." About her inability to tamp down that part of her identity, Hatmaker writes, "I am entirely wired to see, lament, and confront injustice. This is not a thing I do. *This is who I am*" (emphasis mine).[7] I want to analyze what Brown and Hatmaker are saying here, but first I'd like to make an observation. I have seen a few progressive Christian leaders refer to themselves as "prophetic." On a certain level I get what they're saying. They think they're speaking truth to power. Yet it must be said that if your books are being fangirled by celebrities and touted as the latest and greatest self-help miracle and topping the *New York Times* bestseller list, chances are you're not being prophetic. And if the vast majority of a godless culture loves your message, chances are you're not being prophetic. In the Gospel of Luke, Jesus said, "Woe to you, when all people speak well of you, for so their fathers did to the false prophets" (6:26). They killed the prophets. They adore influencers who sanctify sin. True prophets always stood against sin and called people to repent, which often led to the real prophets being persecuted or killed. It was the false prophets who went around giving people counterfeit peace and assurance that everything was fine and that God wouldn't *really* judge them (Jeremiah 6:13-14).

Now let's unpack Brown's statement. She articulates that you are equipped to share your most authentic self with the world by "believing in and belonging to yourself." What is the foundation she is calling her readers to build on? Remember the introduction where we talked about building your house on the rock and not the sand? To get authenticity right, we must build on a solid foundation.

When we see the self as our foundation, as Brown seems to be advocating, we are building on a shifting surface, vulnerable to whatever current positive affirmation sounds right to our most "authentic" selves in the moment. Of course, I realize that one of the most controversial things you can say on social media in America right now is, "My self is broken." I know. I get it. We are not supposed to say that. We are supposed to say we're beautiful, innocent, unbroken, enough, and perfect all by our own adorable little selves. You'll never land a Netflix special with the message "I am broken." But how is that working out for us? You'd think if all we had to do was tap into our inner gods and goddesses, social media would be a much friendlier place, wouldn't it?

This brings us back around to Hatmaker's quote: "I am entirely wired to see, lament, and confront injustice. This is not a thing I do. *This is who I am.*" Seeing, lamenting, and confronting injustice are good things, right? Absolutely. *Unless* we've divorced ourselves from a biblical definition of justice and begun to trust our *own* definition. God condemns injustice at every turn. It goes against his nature and character. God is just. Considering it's one of his attributes, we had better define it the way he does. God's justice is the same as his righteousness. In fact, even though in English *righteousness* and *justice* are two different words, they are translated from the same word group in Hebrew and Greek.[8] In other words, they describe the same attribute of God.

Since biblical justice starts with God's nature and character and not our own inner sense of right and wrong, how we define right and wrong will ultimately determine whether or not the justice we are pursuing in our world is biblical. The current cultural definition of justice is a reflection of what the world (or your own heart) is telling you is good, moral, and true. Biblical justice is a reflection of what God says is good, moral, and true. These are two very different things, and they can often be opposites! If we define justice as our culture currently does, we may end up violating God's definition of justice when we are advocating for something he calls evil or condemning something he calls good. Can you see how an unbiblical definition of justice can default into actual *injustice*? Can you see how basing your identity on your own broken instincts can be a dangerous game?

In the introduction to *Fierce, Free, and Full of Fire*, Hatmaker writes that she finally knows who she is, which positions her to help her readers find out who they are. She celebrates that her outside finally matches her inside "without posturing, posing, or pretending."[9] This sets up a theme that is threaded throughout the book: You can either be real about your own desires, inclinations, and true self *or* you can be a fake, a pushover, or a passive spectator of your own life. This is a false dichotomy, but I can see why it is so appealing. No one wants to be a poser or a doormat. Don't we all want our outsides to match our insides?

The subtle problem with this methodology is that our "insides" aren't always right about things like morality, sexuality, or the definitions of words like *love* and *justice*. As Christians, we have to submit our inner lives to the authority of Scripture, and sometimes that requires denying our desires, repenting of our sinful proclivities, and reforming our ideas to align with God's revealed truth. When we don't do that, we can find ourselves fighting against God and trying to build our identities on a cracked foundation.

## AUTHENTIC SELF-LOVE

Here's the good news. When we make Christ the foundation of everything, the self will fall naturally into its rightful place, which will free us to live in real authenticity. Take, for a practical example, the concept of self-love. With the self as the foundation, our "self-love" will quickly become self-loathing.

I can't love myself if I'm fooling myself about who I actually am. If I deny that there is something wrong with humanity (and thus, myself), the kind of love I will offer myself will be the opposite of authentic. It will be artificial authenticity. I might even recognize my sin, but without a Christ-centered understanding of the Atonement, there will be no mechanism for me to be cleansed, forgiven, and released from the guilt and shame of my sinful actions. My only options will be to give myself a free pass (which won't speak to the guilt), accept my sin as a part of my identity (which will only make things worse), or accept responsibility, apologize, and try to do better. This last one is a start, but with self as the foundation, it only goes so far. Sure, it may smooth things over if you snapped at a friend or stole your sister's favorite jeans for a couple of weeks. No harm, no foul. But what about when someone inflicts egregious evil on another person? If someone attacks another person in a park, steals their wallet, beats them, and leaves them for dead, it won't be enough for the offender to apologize and offer to do better. They can take all the responsibility in the world and become a model citizen, but they're still going to jail. The only way to be truly free from the sin that distorts the image of God in each of us is to repent and trust in Jesus. We will be left with insecurity and even self-loathing if we fail to recognize and accept the cleansing nature of Jesus' death on the cross.

This doesn't mean we shouldn't recognize, celebrate, and grow in the unique gifts and talents God has given us. But it means we should orient those characteristics toward God's holiness. When holiness is the goal, our strengths become refined and intensified. However, when authenticity is the main goal, our strengths can quickly become weaknesses.

In her book *8 Great Smarts: Discover and Nurture Your Child's Intelligences*, Kathy Koch wisely observed: "There is a very fine line between our strengths and our sins."[10] She uses this example: If someone is good with words and with people, they can use those strengths to motivate others if they are pursuing holiness. But they can also use those strengths to *manipulate* others if they are simply pursuing authenticity. This is where biblical authenticity becomes so important. We live in a culture in which people want to determine their own truth and then live "authentically" out of their self-styled identity. But our true authentic identities are God-determined, not self-determined. Our perceptions of our authentic identities must be grounded in Scripture or we run the risk of sinning out of a genuine strength and missing the bull's-eye of what we were created for.

## AUTHENTICITY ISN'T EVERYTHING

The lie we are discussing in this chapter is that authenticity is everything. Authenticity is not unimportant. It's not wrong when defined correctly, but it's not *everything*. Do you want to know what is everything? God's holiness. That's everything.

The word *holiness* has to do with separation. It means that God can have no unity with sin and is entirely separate from it. In the Bible, the root of the Hebrew and Greek words that are translated into English as *holiness* means "to cut or separate."[11] But holiness is not just about God being separate from sin; it's also about his absolute perfection. Theologian Louis Berkhof put it like this: "The idea of ethical holiness is not merely negative (separation from sin); it also has a positive content, namely, that of moral excellence, or ethical perfection."[12]

One of the realities of being a Christian is a process called sanctification. *Sanctify* means to be set apart.[13] Essentially, sanctification is a process that begins at conversion and will continue until it is completed in heaven. It's where we are made more and more like Christ every day, pursuing God's holiness in our own lives. In other words, we are daily being transformed into his image by the renewing of our minds (Romans 12:2). First John 1:7 tells us, "If we walk in the light, as he is in the light, we have fellowship with one another, and the blood of Jesus his Son cleanses us from all sin." Theologian Charles Ryrie described sanctification as the perfect solution to the conundrum of sin versus perfection. As Christians, we can't live up to sinless perfection, nor have we been given a free pass to live it up and sin as we please. Rather, we are to *walk in the light*. Ryrie explained it like this:

> As we respond to increasing light, we will receive more
> light, and so on. But at each stage the requirement is
> the same—walk in the light.
>     To sum up: The standard is God's holiness. The
> requirement is to walk in the light. Our experience
> should always be a growing one, growing to maturity.
> That is true biblical perfectionism.[14]

Anglican scholar Stephen Neill described walking in the light as "absolute sincerity . . . to have nothing to conceal, and to make no attempt to conceal anything."[15] Walking in the light means that we are completely open and honest before God, allowing the shadowed parts of our hearts, desires, thoughts, and inner lives to be laid bare and exposed before the bright beam of his convicting power. Then we respond in humility, confession, repentance, and thankfulness as he continues to illuminate, convict, and nudge us toward holiness.

This is sanctification. To live out biblical authenticity is to celebrate the beauty of the unique gifts, talents, and personalities that God created in each of us. But it is also to acknowledge that sin has marred those traits, and without the cleansing blood of Christ, our particular strengths can be turned into sinful weapons. Being biblically authentic doesn't mean we wink at our sin, celebrate our sin, or give up because of our sin. It means we expose every dark nook and cranny of our hearts to the light and live there. We face our sin, repent, and seek to conform ourselves more to the image of Christ day by day.

## GO AHEAD AND GIVE UP ON YOUR DREAMS

I've given up on two dreams in my life: becoming a gymnast and a singer-songwriter. Both of these vocations were deeply rooted in what I determined was my identity. But I was wrong. My identity is not what I do, what I feel, who I love, who I'm attracted to, or what I think will satisfy me. My identity is who the Bible tells me I am . . . it's who I am in Christ. And his Spirit bears witness with my spirit that *I am a child of God* (Romans 8:16). That knowledge is so freeing because it means that no matter what happens to my physical body or my metaphysical imagination, I am his and he is mine. It means that no matter where I am geographically, what I feel emotionally, what I know intellectually, or what my limitations are physically, I can commune with God and glorify him in whatever situation he puts me in. What freedom.

God had a dream for me I could have never dreamed for myself. For most of my life, I thought my identity was singer-songwriter. I deeply believed that if I could not sing for Jesus, I would miss the purpose of my life. But God, in his unfathomable and vast mercy, took that dream away. I thank Jesus he had a better dream. He providentially placed me in a class that would shake my faith and cause me to study like I had never studied before. (This is a journey I chronicle in my book *Another Gospel? A Lifelong Christian Seeks Truth in Response to Progressive Christianity*.) He opened doors for me to help others with their doubts and questions. He led me to start a blog, which turned into a podcast, which turned into a book, which turned into a YouTube channel, which turned into another book. I didn't see any of it coming. I could not have foreseen feeling more fulfilled and satisfied in my identity as a child of God than I ever possibly could have as a musician. Because my identity is not what I do. It's who I am. I am a child of God whether I sing or write or am silenced by sickness and disease. Today I write. Maybe tomorrow I will wash feet, clean toilets, or start a food blog. God knows. He is trustworthy. My identity is grounded in him. True biblical authenticity is glorifying Christ with whatever gifts and talents he has given me. As my friend Teasi says, this is my calling whether I find myself in a palace or in a prison.[16]

It's no surprise that the world at large tells us to dig inside to discover our authentic selves; after all, it assumes that this life is all we're living for. Knowing who we are in Christ and living in biblical authenticity is a gift that can be brought into focus only when we have an eternal perspective. Life here on earth is temporary. It's a blip on the radar of eternity. With that in mind, shouldn't we "live it up" now? After all, we only get one life, right? Sort of . . .

# NEW YORK

### You Only Have One Life

There are more things in heaven and earth,
Horatio, than are dreamt of in your philosophy.

William Shakespeare, *Hamlet*, Act 1, Scene 5

Oh, New York. I've been in love with the city that never sleeps since my fourteen-year-old self first stepped off the plane at JFK International Airport in the summer of 1989. It was overcast that day—dreary by most standards—but the bleak atmosphere only intensified the fireworks show of stimuli that engaged every one of my senses. The first thing to catch my attention was the thick, humid air that seemed to make every unfamiliar smell come together like an oddly satisfying bouquet of possibility. It smelled like hope. And dirt. And body odors. And perfume and exhaust and something else I've never quite been able to describe with words. It's an aroma unique to New York that I had never smelled before and have never smelled anywhere else. Maybe it's the scent of earth and minerals refusing to be snuffed out by decades of buildings, cars, and people. In New York, smog, gasoline, and rusted steel compete with hot knishes, fresh baked bread, and candied nuts for olfactory domination. If irony were an odor, that would be it—all the best and worst of human progress in one whiff.

The salt of the Atlantic Ocean punched through the air with a zing I could taste on my tongue. The handrail guiding me toward the car park felt slightly damp due to the muggy weather, and I could smell the wet metal that was peeking through the blistered and peeling yellow paint. Honking horns, blaring boom boxes, and the constant chatter of more people than is reasonable for such a small place became the soundtrack of my memories there. I loved every last bit of it. Bob Dylan described his first trip to New York City this way: "Outside the wind was blowing, straggling cloud wisps, snow whirling in the red lanterned streets, city types scuffling around, bundled up—salesmen in rabbit fur earmuffs hawking gimmicks, chestnut vendors, steam rising out of manholes."[1] He experienced the Big Apple in a winter decades before I arrived, but its soul had remained unchanged even in the heat of summer.

I loved the diversity. People from all over the world—from every tribe, nation, and tongue—call New York home. Individuals from all different perspectives, religions, and philosophies are packed side by side and on top of each other in buildings that have nowhere to go but up. Some cities grow to the north or south, but New York grows up to the sky. I loved the no-nonsense and straightforward honesty of New

Yorkers who had zero tolerance for small talk or meaningless pleasantries—#aintnobodygottimeforthat. Some people say New Yorkers are rude. Even as a relatively naive and well-mannered adolescent, I found them delightfully forthright.

Not seven years later my twenty-one-year-old self stepped off the plane at JFK once again. This time, I wasn't there to visit but to stay for almost two life-altering years. I had been invited to help a small church on the Lower East Side minister to neighborhood kids by opening a youth center. We offered an after-school program for young people who were mostly being raised by working single moms. It was a joy to tutor, lead, and love on these kids who, by the way, were some of the smartest and most creative people I've ever known. When someone doesn't have the resources to purchase every latest trendy toy to hit the market, they are forced to create their own amusements. I remember one game in which the kids weighted bottle caps down with chewed gum and flicked the caps back and forth trying to knock their opponent out of a rock-drawn ring.

I loved these kids. But between leading worship a couple of times a week, working another part-time job, fulfilling the demands of the youth center every weekday, and helping out with other church activities and outreaches, I burned myself out very quickly.

To this day, every once in a while I have a recurring dream about New York while I'm in the deepest stages of sleep. The dream is always the same. I am walking down a street. I'm not sure which one, but in the dream it's so familiar. I can taste, touch, smell, see, and hear it. But I can't remember the name. Is it Houston? Bleeker? Broadway? Second Avenue? Goodness . . . which one is it? I can never quite identify it. I start walking down the street that I can't name while looking for a house I can't reach. It's a small apartment somewhere south of Soho, but where? I'm not sure. I can't remember. When I think about it, I see beautiful shades of yellow and orange, and it feels like home and family, warmth and food, security, music, love, and comfort all wrapped into one. But I can never find it. Why can't I remember where it is? I always end up wandering along the street until I give up or wake up. The house eludes me every time. I never find it. Sometimes I get close. One time I even saw the front door, a raw umber rectangle at the top of some iron steps ascending from a coffee shop on the corner. But I can never quite get there. Whenever I get close, time slows down, my arms and legs become heavy, and it becomes almost impossible to move. I try to put one foot in front of the other, but it's like they are lodged in wet cement. Somehow in this dream, I know that if I can ever get there, I'll be home. There will be no more tears or sorrow or pain. This is where the unbroken live.

## #YOLO

Have more fun. Do what makes you happy. Wear Crocs to prom. Buy Girl Scout cookies. Overpay for tacos. Indulge in that decadent dessert. Drink that extra cocktail. Buy those overpriced sneakers. Pull the trigger on that new sports car. Hike that mountain. Avoid the big pile of clothes in your laundry room. Pay for that marathon. Decide that you would pay money to *not* run a marathon. A quick search of the #YOLO (you only live once) hashtag on social media will provide many statements like the ones above. Some are hilarious. Some are more serious. Some are good and healthy, while some are unhelpful, sinful, and toxic. What's the one thing all these statements have in common, though? Motive. The *reason* behind the *why* and *what* is the same. The rationale behind the idea that you only live once is this: There are no eternal consequences for our choices. When we die, that's it. Lights out. Might as well empty our savings accounts and book that luxury vacation we've been dreaming about. Why not, right?

I was smacked in the face with this idea one night when a television commercial came on during my favorite prime-time show. It began with a confusingly happy song playing underneath a funeral procession in which a sad-looking young man marched through the snow as another man looked at his watch. (Because funerals are so boring?) The scene cut to a car skidding away from the graveside as the young man with the watch drove to a trendy exclusive club filled with live music, liquor, and beautiful women. A song blaring above the dancing, drinking, laughing, and flirting urged the revelers to have fun; "it's later than you think." Then the slogan, "You have a single life" flashed on the screen as the product, a single-malt whiskey, came into focus. The clear message of the ad was that nothing will remind you of your own mortality more clearly than a funeral, and at some point, every one of us will be in that casket. One day you'll be six feet underground, so live it up. Because #YOLO.

## VAMPIRE NOVOCAIN

As we have already observed, materials that emphasize self-reliance and autonomy sell like hotcakes because they sound positive on the surface. But when you really think about it, they are kind of like Alec the vampire's superpower in Stephenie Meyer's smash-hit book series, The Twilight Saga. I have a confession to make. I read *Twilight* when it first came out, convincing myself it was for "research purposes"—you know, to find out what kids were into these days. In reality, I was completely hooked by the unusual story line and mythology of the Cullen universe. Never mind the fact that the story is based on a love triangle between a broody 104-year-old vampire, a clumsy and moody 17-year-old girl with no discernible talents or life goals, and a sweet-natured but rowdy young werewolf. It was *Beauty and the Beast* on steroids.

In the Twilight world, each vampire possesses a special ability that is unique to them. Edward can read minds, Jasper can control people's moods, Alice can see the future, and Jane can incapacitate others with intense physical pain. Then there's Alec. Alec can manifest a mist-like fog that creeps up on people and slowly shuts off their senses, even paralyzing them at his will. His particular gift could be used to kill enemies without them even realizing what is happening.

At the end of The Twilight Saga, there is a confrontation between the Cullen family and the Volturi, a type of vampire royalty. Alec, a Volturi, dispatches the mist to render the Cullens powerless and more easily controlled. But not so fast. Enter Bella Cullen, whose superpower happens to be creating a mental shield around others, cutting off the influence of certain types of powers. She wraps a bubble of protection around her family, and when the mist reaches it, she remarks, "I could taste it as soon as it touched my shield—it had a dense, sweet, cloying flavor. It made me remember dimly the numbness of Novocain on my tongue."[2]

It's not difficult to see the comparison here. The enchanting fog that tells us, "You only have one life" numbs us to thoughts about our eternal destination. Like Alec's mist, there is a subtle and heavy sweetness to it. It's intoxicating. If we can shut off our senses from the impending reality of heaven, hell, and final judgment, we can be free to pursue our best lives now. We can justify all manner of fun and frivolity, pleasure and purchase because, you know, #YOLO.

## OUT OF THIS WORLD

As Christians, we are not supposed to think this way. Jesus wants our hearts to be focused on heaven, not earth. In Matthew 6:19-21, Jesus teaches that the only place we should store up treasures for ourselves is in heaven. Anything we build for this world can be stolen, broken, or ruined. He emphasizes, "Where your treasure is, there your heart will be also." In John 17:14, when Jesus is praying for his disciples, he notes that the world hates them because they are "not of the world," just as he is not of the world. In John 15:18-19, Jesus, while speaking to his disciples during the Last Supper, explains that if we identify with those who oppose him (the world), they will love us, but if we follow Christ, they will hate us. Jesus focuses on eternity in John 18:36 when he declares, "My kingdom is not of this world." He warns, "For what will it profit a man if he gains the whole world and forfeits his soul?" and goes on to state that he will return to "repay each person according to what he has done" (Matthew 16:26-27).

In Philippians 3:12-21, the apostle Paul builds on this idea. He urges Christians to think in terms of pressing "on toward the goal for the prize of the upward call of God in Christ Jesus" (verse 14). He reminds us that our primary citizenship is not to a country, state, or city on earth: "Our citizenship is in heaven, and from it we await a Savior, the Lord Jesus Christ, who will transform our lowly body to be like his glorious body, by the power that enables him even to subject all things to himself" (verses 20-21).

It can be jarring to reorient our thinking this way, especially if we are not used to considering ourselves "exiles" on earth, as the apostle Peter refers to Christians. In 1 Peter 2:9-12, he writes that we have been chosen and are God's own possession. This does not mean God intends for us to be miserable or that we are to withhold good things from ourselves while on earth. Rather, Peter explains that we see ourselves as exiles so that we may "proclaim the excellencies of him who called [us] out of darkness into his marvelous light" (verse 9). In other words, we have great news to share about a much better world that God is inviting us into. With that in mind, Peter urges Christ followers to keep ourselves from sinful passions that are at war with our souls.

Does this mean we shouldn't enjoy our lives or ever

indulge in good food, fun, and celebration? Certainly not! We aren't talking about biding our time on earth until we can escape to heaven. It means that our eyes should be fixed on our eternal home, the Kingdom of God. David described this Kingdom beautifully about a thousand years before Jesus did: "You make known to me the path of life; in your presence there is fullness of joy; at your right hand are pleasures forevermore" (Psalm 16:11). His Kingdom is immeasurably better than the pleasure we get from a temporary shopper's high, sugar fix, or adrenaline rush. Heaven isn't a weird and supernatural place where angels sit on clouds with harps. It's our home. Philosopher Peter Kreeft put it this way:

> Home—that's what heaven is. It won't appear strange and faraway and "supernatural", but utterly natural. Heaven is what we were designed for. All our epics seek it: It is the "home" of Odysseus, of Aeneas, of Frodo, of E. T. Heaven is not escapist. Worldliness is escapist. Heaven is home.[3]

## LET'S COMPARE

Now that we've taken a peek into the soul-satisfying Kingdom we are citizens of, let's compare what the Bible says with what some popular authors and teachers are saying in resources marketed to Christians:

> Dear reader, YOU ONLY HAVE ONE LIFE TO LIVE. What if you die tomorrow having never given your dream a shot?[4]

I'm a big fan of displaying visuals inside my closet
door to remind me every single day of what my aim
is. Currently taped to my door: the cover of *Forbes*
featuring self-made female CEOs, a vacation house
in Hawaii . . . and a picture of Beyoncé, obvi.[5]

These quotations reveal how a #YOLO mentality is quite selfish in nature, and is focused only on the here and now rather than the eternal. But what a joy to know that even if you never fulfill that dream you've had since you were a kid, you have a much better life to look forward to. And even if you did somehow achieve that dream, it doesn't compare to the joy that waits for you in heaven. Even if you never buy that vacation house, get that dream job, receive that promotion, or fit into those jeans, this life is not the main event. This perspective is also helpful when you have to deny yourself and obey Christ even when it hurts—when his commands get all up in your business and make you uncomfortable.

Jesus' brother James gives wise advice in James 4:14: "You do not know what tomorrow will bring. What is your life? For you are a mist that appears for a little time and then vanishes." And take a moment to ponder these words of Paul and his companions *after* Paul had been stoned and left for dead for preaching the gospel: "Through many tribulations we must enter the kingdom of God" (Acts 14:22).

What does this all have to do with an apartment in New York I can never find? Literally everything. I long for the heart-soothing warmth of that unfindable home because my soul longs for something that is actually *real*. It's kind of like hunger and thirst. Our bodies experience a need for food and drink *because* there is a real object that satisfies these desires. Think about it. Would your body experience thirst if water didn't exist? Would it hunger if food were not a reality?[6] We all have a deep sense of unrealized goals, unrequited love, and unfulfilled dreams because the object of these desires is real, even if it's not fully actualized in this life. How exciting is that?

When I wake up with that empty feeling, that ache of disappointment, that pit in my stomach, I know that what I'm really longing for is something no earthly apartment can live up to. I long for heaven. Even if all the hopes I have for my life here on earth are never within my grasp, I know that something so much more beautiful, fulfilling, and wonderful is waiting for me on the other side. And even if I were to somehow manage to achieve everything I could put my mind to on this earth, it would pale in comparison with the absolute ecstasy of being fully enveloped in the love of God forever.

But this is a hard sell in a world that has turned God into a magical vending machine, doling out all the goodies our little hearts desire. This brings us to another lie that we must unravel if we are to really get this into our bones. I hate to be the one to say it, but God's ultimate goal for you isn't your happiness.

8

# MOSQUITOES

God Just Wants You to Be Happy

They seemed to be staring at the dark,
but their eyes were watching God.

Zora Neale Hurston, *Their Eyes Were Watching God*

My friend Médine survived a long, grueling year and a half as a refugee after a civil war broke out in her native Congo. With her home city of Dolisie in flames behind her, she strapped her sixteen-month-old son, David, to her back and set out with her family to survive what would be eighteen months of homelessness, malnutrition, thirst, disease, hostile villagers, gunfire, and the never-ceasing danger of roving militias and gangs. With no international supply lines to bring help or provisions, Médine and her family were forced to trek through forested areas on feet bruised from stone-capped terrain in order to find food and shelter. No one had proper shoes. There was no medicine. Food was scarce, and clean water was rare. The water they could find was usually dirty and contaminated, which made dysentery a daily reality.

Often Médine had to walk more than six miles in the scorching sun to forage for cassava roots she would harvest, bring back to her family, cook, and then serve as their one meal for the day. Médine remembers:

> Most often, to reach the cassava fields, we had to pass through streams of army ants. Some of the ants would drop from the trees onto us; others would climb our legs. We would have to strip and pick off the ants; we could brush off the ants' bodies, killing them, but we still had to remove their mandibles from our skin.[1]

(Pro tip: Next time one of your friends complains about something trivial, just ask them, "But did you have to remove *ant mandibles* from your skin?") Sometimes they had to eat rats for protein. Nights were spent on dirt floors with no blankets, huddled and shivering before the whole process of hiking for miles, drinking dirty water, and scavenging for food began again. It was especially difficult for the women, who were under constant threat of sexual assault. As Médine put it, "Rape was a frequent weapon of war."[2]

If that all wasn't enough, one of the most consistent hazards they faced was malaria. The people were hungry, but the mosquitoes were hungrier. With mosquitoes outnumbering people by about a bajillion to one, Médine and her family became a nonstop meal for these ravenous pests. I cannot imagine what it was like for her, waking up in the night and seeing her baby's head so covered with bites that it looked like he'd grown a full head of hair overnight. She and David both contracted malaria more than once. David nearly died. Many people did.

## THE POVERTY OF PROSPERITY

Médine's harrowing story represents the level of adversity that many people in the world have endured throughout history. It may seem shocking to those of us who eat three meals a day and have access to clean water, clothes, shoes, shelter, and bug spray, but until more modern times and the rise of Western civilization, life was pretty hard for everyone. Christians expected hardships. They assumed that even though this life was fraught with suffering, they had a God who walked with them in this world, offering a future hope of eternal bliss in the next. But something happened in recent history that tossed the narrative upside down. We got rich. We became affluent and confident. We no longer needed to depend on God every single second of every day because we had coats to keep us warm and cars to drive us to the jobs that earned us money to spend on groceries, clothes, and modern medicine. These are all good things. I'm thankful for them—especially modern medicine and the invention of anesthesia. Can we all just take a moment and thank the good Lord for anesthesia?

But there is a certain poverty that arises out of prosperity. We tend to forget the real purpose of life. Remember what that is? To worship God and enjoy him forever. We are made in his image, after all. The closer we are to him, the more truly happy we will be. But when we have a veritable smorgasbord of comforts and possessions to distract us from our true spiritual need, we have to make a conscious effort to remind ourselves of how dependent we are on God. This is why it is not always his highest goal to make us comfy and happy on earth. As we'll see, trials are a gift.

### A new cultural religion

Beginning in 2001, sociologist Christian Smith led a team of researchers with the National Study of Youth and Religion, who assessed the spiritual beliefs of the average American teenager. After interviewing more than three thousand teens, they identified five beliefs the typical teen had in common:

1. A God exists who created and orders the world and watches over human life on earth.
2. God wants people to be good, nice, and fair to each other, as taught in the Bible and by most world religions.
3. The central goal of life is to be happy and to feel good about oneself.
4. God does not need to be particularly involved in one's life except when God is needed to resolve a problem.
5. Good people go to heaven when they die.[3]

Smith and his team summed up these beliefs by coining a new phrase: moralistic therapeutic deism. Basically, American teenagers were under the impression that God just wanted them to be happy and nice to one another. This kindhearted therapist in the sky would grant their wishes if they needed anything but would otherwise keep his distance. He certainly wouldn't butt into their sex lives or ask them to do anything that made them feel sad, uncomfortable, or deprived. For those with this mentality, the self becomes the center of the universe. Now that all those teenagers are adults, this belief system has permeated all parts of society. We've bought into this one hook, line and sinker.

## GOD ACTUALLY *DOES* WANT YOU TO BE HAPPY . . .

When we interpret the Bible properly, we discover . . . surprise! It's actually not a lie that God wants you to be happy . . . depending on how you characterize *happiness*. Many people today define happiness as a psychological state of contentment. It's the good feeling you have when you sip a rich cup of coffee or appreciate a beautiful sunset. Popular culture tells us that happiness means controlling our circumstances in a way that allows us to have those good feelings as often as possible, and if we don't experience those good feelings, we should change our circumstances. Are you unhappy in your marriage? Get a divorce. Feeling down? Get drunk. Overwhelmed by motherhood? Take to social media to vent about what little monsters your kids are. The problem: Those types of emotions and behaviors are fleeting and situational. Changing our circumstances sometimes makes us feel better in the moment but can damage ourselves and others in the long run.

The Bible defines happiness in a completely different way. It's not a psychological state or an emotion we experience. It's described more like an alignment with God and obedience to his Word. It's a God-focused joy, not a self-centered mood enhancement. Consider Acts 5:17-42, when the apostles were arrested by the religious leaders and put in prison for preaching the gospel and healing people. An angel miraculously let them out of jail and told them to go directly to the Temple and preach. They obeyed, which provoked the religious leaders to have them flogged with a warning to stop speaking in the name of Jesus. Put yourself in the disciples' place for a moment. How would you respond? I hate to admit that I would probably question the goodness of God for a moment. I might think something like, *Really, God? You sent an angel to literally escort me out of prison, and then when I do what the angel told me to do, I get beaten up and threatened? How does that make any sense?* I would be responding out of self-focus, not God-focus.

But how does the Bible say the apostles responded? They "left the presence of the council, rejoicing that they were counted worthy to suffer dishonor for the name" (verse 41). How could this be? What did they know that we struggle to get through our thick skulls sometimes? I think they understood what true happiness is. Biblical happiness doesn't come from having stuff, feeling good about our circumstances, or even finding romantic fulfillment. Those things *feel* good, but they can't bring ultimate happiness. In some cases, they may even distract us from real happiness. True biblical happiness is knowing deep down that no matter our circumstances, we were lost and now we're found. We have experienced the love of Christ, which always brings encouragement and comfort. According to our culture, this makes no sense, but in God's wisdom, it's perfect. This must be why the apostle Paul was able to express true happiness despite being threatened with death: "Even if I am to be poured out as a drink offering upon the sacrificial offering of your faith, I am glad and rejoice with you all. Likewise you also should be glad and rejoice with me" (Philippians 2:17-18).

## ...BUT GOD MOSTLY WANTS YOU TO BE OBEDIENT

It's no wonder Paul was able to rejoice under trying circumstances. He flipped suffering on its head. In the biblical paradigm, suffering isn't pitted against happiness; they go hand in hand. During his ministry Paul endured hunger, thirst, and cold. He was kidnapped, beaten, whipped, imprisoned, ridiculed, shipwrecked, and stoned—all before he was finally beheaded. In Romans 8:38-39, he reminds us that nothing can separate us from the love of Christ, specifically mentioning tribulation, distress, persecution, nakedness, famine, danger, and the sword.

Paul was such an expert in suffering, he even pleaded with God to take away a mysterious "thorn . . . in the flesh." Whatever this particular affliction was, he described it as "a messenger of Satan to harass me" and begged God three times to take it away (2 Corinthians 12:7-8). The answer was a clear no. God told him his grace was sufficient. So Paul decided that he would boast in his weaknesses. He gloriously declared,

"For the sake of Christ, then, I am content with weaknesses, insults, hardships, persecutions, and calamities. For when I am weak, then I am strong" (verse 10). This wasn't Paul simply looking on the bright side or keeping a cheery outlook like Pollyanna playing the glad game in the famous Disney movie. This is a man who recognized the deep benefit and ultimate gift that suffering is in the life of a Christian. Paul understood that to be truly happy, you're going to have to get comfortable with suffering. From a prison cell, he wrote these words to the believers in Philippi: "It has been granted to you that for the sake of Christ you should not only believe in him but also suffer for his sake" (Philippians 1:29).

Okay. Let's pause for a second. Paul might sound like a glutton for punishment or some kind of masochist. Quite the opposite. Paul is helping us understand that the minor hardships we experience in this life are getting us ready for eternity. In the economy of heaven, suffering actually produces joy. Remember Elisabeth Elliot from chapter 5, who lived as a missionary among the very tribe that killed her husband? Joni Eareckson Tada recounts meeting her many years later as the two of them were speaking at a conference together. Joni, paralyzed from the neck down as a result of a diving accident in her teens, also knew a thing or two about suffering. She recalls the meeting fondly: "We were simply followers of Christ who had plumbed the depths of His joy by tasting His afflictions. Those afflictions had cut deep gashes in our hearts through which grace and joy had poured in, stretching and filling our souls with an abundance of our Lord."[4]

## HUNGER IS THE BEST SEASONING

Have you ever thought about how the hungrier you are the better food tastes? Have you wondered why cold water is so much more satisfying when your throat burns with thirst? Let's apply that to happiness. What about pain? Think about the worst physical pain you've ever experienced. For me, it was childbirth. Until I experienced it, I didn't even have a mental category for that level of agony. The minute my daughter was born, however, the pain ceased and my entire body was deluged with the most astonishing and euphoric relief. Without the misery, I would not have a mental category for that level of elation.

That's an extreme example, but take the classic tale *Charlie and the Chocolate Factory*. I read the book as a kid and loved the 1971 movie version in which Gene Wilder utterly nailed the character of Willy Wonka. (Can we all take a moment of silence to mourn the disaster that was the 2005 version starring Johnny Depp? Sorry, Johnny. You make a great pirate and I loved you as Edward Scissorhands, but it's a hard pass on your Wonka.) As the story goes, the character of Veruca Salt is a spoiled little brat who manipulates her parents into buying her whatever she wants simply by screaming. Charlie, on the other hand, is a humble and kind boy so poor he survives on cabbage soup and doesn't even own a winter coat. Once a year, he receives a chocolate bar for his birthday. He savors every tiny nibble, often making the bar last for over a month.

A contest is announced in which a handful of lucky winners will get to tour the mysterious chocolate factory and meet the eccentric owner, Willy Wonka. Five golden tickets are hidden in the wrappers of candy bars shipped all over the world. Veruca tantrums her way into coercing her dad to buy a half a million of them and redirect the workers of his factory to unwrap them one by one until she has her golden ticket. Three other unlikable children strike gold as well. Only one unclaimed ticket remains. Charlie's single hope is his upcoming birthday chocolate bar. He's got one shot. He slowly peels back one corner of the Whipple-Scrumptious Fudgemallow Delight bar that he gratefully accepted as a birthday gift from his destitute parents. Even though the golden ticket is not inside, he offers the first bite to his mother and invites all of his family members to share in the bounty. Veruca, on the other hand, doesn't appreciate even one of the candy bars. There is no thankfulness or humility. Only entitlement and discontent. Charlie relishes each bite with such delight because he had lived through the most excruciating pangs of hunger.

(Author's note: Since writing the first draft of this book, I have reread *Charlie and the Chocolate Factory* and rewatched both movies. I am not ashamed to admit I was wrong. Johnny Depp was a brilliant Willy Wonka and captured the vision of the character with a nuance Gene Wilder failed to execute. From his boyish high-pitched voice to his dark and pointed sarcasm, Depp embodied the book version. And bonus points for the evil dentist-dad backstory. You see, I only thought Gene Wilder nailed it because his Wonka was all I knew. I have since deconstructed that nonsense. I have done the work. I will do better. Moving on.)

## BACK TO PAUL

Now that we understand the practical angle of how suffering helps develop character, we turn back to Paul, who put it this way in Romans 5:3-5: "We rejoice in our sufferings, knowing that suffering produces endurance, and endurance produces character, and character produces hope, and hope does not put us to shame, because God's love has been poured into our hearts through the Holy Spirit who has been given to us." According to Paul, suffering is something we should actually *rejoice* in. James agrees: "Count it all joy, my brothers, when you meet trials of various kinds, for you know that the testing of your faith produces steadfastness" (James 1:2-3). The apostle Peter tells us, "Beloved, do not be surprised at the fiery trial when it comes upon you to test you, as though something strange were happening to you. But rejoice insofar as you share Christ's sufferings, that you may also rejoice and be glad when his glory is revealed" (1 Peter 4:12-13).

Allowing God to use our suffering to strengthen our character, deepen our joy, and draw us closer to him seems to be a theme throughout the Bible. There's a relationship between human suffering and God's glory being revealed. The psalmist wrote, "It is good for me that I was afflicted, that I might learn your statutes" (Psalm 119:71). Paul's perseverance in suffering also reflects their understanding that this world is not their final destination:

I consider that the sufferings of this present time are not worth comparing with the glory that is to be revealed to us.

ROMANS 8:18

We do not lose heart. Though our outer self is wasting away, our inner self is being renewed day by day. For this light momentary affliction is preparing for us an eternal weight of glory beyond all comparison, as we look not to the things that are seen but to the things that are unseen. For the things that are seen are transient, but the things that are unseen are eternal.

2 CORINTHIANS 4:16-18

## LET'S COMPARE

Compare the words of Paul, James, Peter, and the psalmist with popular thought leaders today:

To say we can learn something from suffering is to give suffering too much value and meaning. Suffering does not transform. Suffering dehumanizes. Suffering is evil.[5]

You, and only you, are ultimately responsible for who you become and how happy you are.[6]

You are allowed to want more for yourself for no other reason than because it makes your heart happy.[7]

## TREASURES DISCOVERED IN THE DARKNESS

For his book *Live Not by Lies*, Rod Dreher interviewed many Christians from the former Soviet bloc who survived intense persecution by a totalitarian regime. What stood out to him more than anything was the deep abiding joy they exuded. He noted that Christians should "accept the impenetrable mystery that suffering, if rightly received, can be a gift."[8]

My friend Médine, whose story opened this chapter, understands this well. As I prepared to write this section, I emailed her with a simple question: "Médine, while you were a refugee, enduring constant sickness, threat of danger, hunger, and thirst, what would you have thought if someone were to say to you, 'God just wants you to be happy'?" With her permission, I share her words:

> Being a Christian is not a Pollyanna syndrome where we are happy all the time. God created us with a range of emotions and on this earth we will experience them. They help us grow into mature, well-balanced human beings. It is easy to wish we will always be happy, but life is not all roses; there are difficult times when we experience sadness and anger and heartbreak and grief. I thank God for times of happiness, but I thank him for difficult times too. All these moments have allowed me to become the person God wants me to be. I have learned valuable lessons during my times as a war refugee and during the loss of my parents and sibling, like treasures discovered in the darkness. I have also learned wonderful lessons when I am happy. God wants us to have a dynamic and intimate relationship

with him that will take us through times of hardship and joy.

As Christians, we aren't supposed to seek out suffering as some kind of self-flagellation. We don't rejoice in suffering for suffering's sake. The purpose of suffering in the life of a Christian is to conform us to the image of Christ. In order to do that, our own personal wants, desires, and dreams have to die. This can be very painful.

## INCOMING
### *How to Assess the Pushback Coming Your Way*

#### Am I being hated or persecuted as a Christian?

### If no, why not?
- [ ] I'm not sure how to stand up for my faith.
- [ ] I'd rather go along to get along with everyone.
- [ ] I don't want to be called a bigot.
- [ ] I don't want to lose something of value (e.g., my reputation, my job).
- [ ] It seems unloving to criticize others' opinions.
- [ ] I spend time almost exclusively with other believers.

### If yes, is it because of
- [ ] my condemnation of immoral behavior?
- [ ] my tone?
- [ ] my name-calling of others?
- [ ] my unwillingness to compromise on essentials?
- [ ] my unwillingness to agree to disagree on nonessentials?
- [ ] my reliance on Scripture as the ultimate authority?

If you are a Christian, you are promised suffering. The apostle Paul wrote, "All who desire to live a godly life in Christ Jesus will be persecuted" (2 Timothy 3:12), and Jesus promised in John 16:33 that "in the world you will have tribulation." He guaranteed in John 15:18-19 that if you are truly following him, the world will hate you as it hated him. One question I continually ask myself is this: Since Paul said *all* true Christians would be persecuted and Jesus promised that the world would hate his true followers, am I seeing that in my life? Am I being hated and persecuted? I certainly don't set out to offend anyone, and I always try to present the gospel in the most loving and persuasive way possible. But even so, does 90 percent of a godless culture just *love* what I post on social media? Or am I sharing in the sufferings of Christ?

Oswald Chambers once wrote, "Are we partakers of Christ's sufferings? Are we prepared for God to stamp out our personal ambitions? Are we prepared for God to destroy our individual decisions by supernaturally transforming them?"[9] That is the question we must all wrestle with. We don't always know why trials come into our lives. We don't know the end of the story like God does. But I'm sure Médine, Elisabeth Elliot, Joni Eareckson Tada, and Christians from the former Soviet bloc would agree with Chambers that with suffering comes an unexpected gift: "Suddenly we come to a place of enlightenment, and realize—'God has strengthened me and I didn't even know it!'"[10]

# MCJUDGYPANTS

## You Shouldn't Judge

Judgment is given to men that they may use it.
Because it may be used erroneously, are men
to be told that they ought not to use it at all?

John Stuart Mill, *On Liberty*

"I'm sorry to be the one to have to say this, girls. But the record label wants you all to lose ten pounds. You'll find a gym membership waiting for each of you when you get home."

My two bandmates and I sat huddled around the speakerphone in a New York hotel room at the end of a short press tour to promote our upcoming first album. Apparently, someone had told the powers that be at our record company about all those hours ZOEgirl had spent in the studio munching on sugary cereal, chips, and candy while rehearsing and recording. Our bad habit had caught up with us, and headquarters had issued a red alert. Since we were a teen-focused pop group who sang and danced, I'm sure the label was concerned that we stay in top shape.

Kind of like the seven stages of grief, we processed this news in phases. First there were eye rolls, then nervous laughter, then shock that turned to hurt, disbelief, sarcasm, and finally anger. We could certainly understand a secular label making this request. But a Christian company? We got to work channeling all of our angsty energy into creating a hand-drawn comic strip, something we often did to cope with the pressures of constant writing, recording, and touring. In this particular installment, we depicted ourselves as morbidly obese pop stars, with fat rolls sprouting out from every seam of our ridiculously tight and tasseled pleather outfits. Like giant human balls, we came rolling back into town only to find that the record label had taken out a billboard ad with an announcement in blinking lights: "ZOEGIRL IS FAT." In that hotel room we guffawed until we cried. I don't know how deeply this affected the other two, but the tears that came at the end of my laughter were deep, bitter, and chaotic. I was utterly spun out.

My mind instantly transported me back to the blue-flower wallpapered bathroom of my childhood home, where I had first tried to make myself throw up when I was about eleven. Not long before, my gymnastics coach had patted my tummy and told me I needed to do extra sit-ups to work off my Thanksgiving feast. That first attempt was a terrible experience, and I never wanted to do it again. But every comment about my weight after that touched an already tender wound.

It wasn't until my early twenties that I gave purging another shot. It was easier this time and happened on occasion, but I still fought against it. By the time I was twenty-five and ZOEgirl was just getting started, I thought I had it under control. But now things had gotten real.

*You need to lose ten pounds.* No matter what I did, I could not get that pronouncement out of my head. I don't blame my gymnastics coach, my record label, or anyone else who may have thrown an offhand comment my way. My life choices are on me. But every remark hurt. When my bandmates and I were told to lose weight, everything in me wanted to respond with maturity and grace, but I had a history of bulimia and a photo shoot coming up. It was the perfect storm.

When we got back to town, we received a friendly invitation to meet up with one of the record company's top-level executives for a Pilates class. (You know, just a casual get-together to do some Pilates. No ulterior motives.) We were invited out for coffee to be educated about all things carbohydrates and assigned a personal health coach. I got the message loud and clear. For the next few years, my life was a consistent cycle of work and more work. When we weren't writing songs, we were recording. When we weren't recording, we were doing interviews. When we weren't doing interviews, we were hopping on a tour bus for weeks at a time to fulfill a soul-crushing performance schedule. When we weren't traveling, we were planning our next album or tour opportunity. For me, prayer and Bible study took a back seat to exhaustion. When I was home for a few precious days, I was mostly alone. I hadn't had the chance to make non-touring friends or connect with a church family after moving to Nashville to join the group. I did try to attend church on

Sundays, but I was acutely aware that I could be recognized. The fact that I had just seen my face blown up to the size of a brontosaurus on a marketing banner downtown made me careful and guarded.

I was never comfortable with fame, regardless of how relatively small my brush with it was. So I would eat. I would binge and then I would purge. Wash. Rinse. Repeat. I was hooked. I was also deeply ashamed of my eating disorder, so I hid it like a dirty little secret. But I wasn't fooling anyone. On some tour in some town somewhere, I shared a hotel room with one of my bandmates. She is a sweetheart— gentle, deeply intelligent, and thoughtful. She is genuinely one of the kindest and warmest people I have ever met. She was also a natural peacemaker, and confrontation did not come easily to her. So when she worked up every last bit of courage to ask me what I was doing in the bathroom, it surprised me. And it also made me angry. To put it lightly, the conversation didn't go well. I not so politely invited her to stop "judging" me and back all the way off. That didn't stop her—#neverthelessshepersisted.

She even involved my other bandmate, and together they lovingly asked me to admit what I was doing so they could help me. That interaction didn't go so well either. It took me a while to come around. But my bandmates' determination to get me help and accountability changed my life. I ended up confessing my secret and getting counseling to begin healing.

Looking back, am I thankful that my bandmate "judged" me? That she dared confront me about the self-harm I was guilty of? Absolutely! She was the catalyst that first brought the darkness into the light. To this day my eyes mist with tears when I think about how much she *loved* me to do such a difficult thing.

## WHY DOES THE LIE "YOU SHOULDN'T JUDGE" SOUND SO GOOD?

Sometimes people refuse to call out bad behavior or ideas because it seems like the loving thing to do. I totally get it. If I just live and let live, never scrutinizing the ideas of pop culture, books, and blogs, I would *feel* like a much more loving person. I've noticed that a lot of people live by this philosophy. I don't know how many times I've heard "It just feels right to me" or "It isn't my place to judge; I only know what's true for me." Unwittingly, people are parroting ideas that simply don't match reality. If you really stop to think about it, saying "Don't judge" doesn't even make sense.

Imagine you are home alone and your doorbell rings. You peek through the window and observe a very large man with a gun in his hand, wearing an orange jumpsuit. He's sweating and looking around nervously. Be honest. Are you going to open the door for him? My guess is . . . probably not. But wait. Why are you being so judgmental? Maybe he's not an escaped convict but simply enjoys wearing orange jumpsuits and carrying his weapon while out for a jog. Who are you to judge?

Obviously, this is an extreme example. No one would open the door for that guy. But this goes to show that *literally everyone judges.* We all make judgments about people every single day. It would be beyond illogical, and sometimes unsafe, to *not* judge.

Plus, to even tell someone they shouldn't judge is to judge that they are judging, which is considered judgmental, which requires making a judgment about all the judging. You get the point.

The word *judgment* has a couple of different connotations. In a courtroom, a judge carries out various duties such as determining liability and damage, sentencing guilty parties, and ruling on the admissibility of evidence. Unless you are an actual judge, you should probably not be doing those things. But in the broader sense of the word, to judge something means to conclude that one thing is better than another.

## DIGITAL COURAGE

"You shouldn't judge" has become a veritable mantra in our culture. When people say it, they generally mean that you should never criticize the moral choices of another person. A few months after I started blogging in 2016, I penned an article called "5 Signs Your Church Might Be Heading toward Progressive Christianity," which was viewed more than 400,000 times in the first few weeks. Until that point, my only serious personal interaction with progressive Christians had been within the confines of a small and exclusive study group at a local church. But now on the internet, where people feel much more freedom to write whatever comes into their heads, I received a crash course in wider progressive thought. If it's true that alcohol gives people "liquid courage" to say things they might not otherwise say, I'm convinced that social media provides "*digital* courage" for people to do the same online.

Here is an excerpt from an email I received in response to my article from a man who was deeply concerned with what he perceived as my "condemnation" of other people's interpretation of Christianity:

> You are responsible for yourself. Being critical of others who do not accept your point of view as the "only way" to the father is pretty narrow minded. That does not mean that everyone is correct in their theology, it just means that they should be respected and allowed to practice their Christianity as they believe. If you disagree, then my advice is simply find another church which you feel is a better fit. And don't forget that little scripture . . . "Judge not, lest you be judged."

A couple of years after that, a wildly popular book written by a self-professed Christian author was released by a Christian publishing house and marketed on Christian platforms. It was a fairy tale come true. Crushing it at the top of the *New York Times* Best Sellers list and winning the hearts and minds of millions of women, *Girl, Wash Your Face* by Rachel Hollis was featured in countless small-group Bible studies and conferences nationwide.

As I read it, I became convinced that the core message

of the book is the exact opposite of the biblical gospel. So I decided to write a review and post it on my blog. I didn't anticipate it going viral, nor did I predict the boatloads of hate mail that would sail into my inbox in the following weeks.

Some of the emails cannot be repeated in polite company. But the bulk of the pushback can be distilled down to three fateful words: "*You. Shouldn't. Judge.*" The message I received loud and clear was that it was wrong of me to criticize unbiblical ideas in a popular book. After all, Jesus would never be such a "McJudgypants."

Several people commented that I should have reached out to Rachel Hollis personally before I called her out. (Interestingly, none of those people contacted me personally before calling me out publicly for calling Hollis out publicly.) But goodness. Should I have just shut my trap and kept my opinions to myself? Surely not. Bad ideas have tangible effects on real people.

In *Girl, Wash Your Face*, Rachel Hollis wrote:

> Just because you believe it doesn't mean it's true for everyone. In so many instances judgment comes from a place of feeling as though you've somehow got it all figured out when they do not. *Judging each other actually makes us feel safer in our own choices.* Faith is one of the most abused instances of this. We decide that our religion is right; therefore, every other religion must be wrong. Within the same religion, or heck, even within the same church, people judge each other for not being the right kind of Christian, Catholic, Mormon, or Jedi.[1]

In all fairness, Hollis follows this up by acknowledging that friends should hold each other accountable. She writes that asking a friend to consider their actions in a certain light flows out of a heart of love. I appreciate that distinction. However, notice that in the context of her quote, Hollis removes this accountability from the realm of objective truth in religion. In other words, it's okay to hold a Christian friend accountable, just as long as that accountability isn't because you've decided your interpretation of Christianity is right and theirs is wrong. As we learned in chapter 3, Christianity cannot be separated from objective truth but is, in fact, dependent upon it. Following this thinking to its logical end, Hollis's definition of accountability implicitly prohibits Christians from confronting each other in their actual sin or false beliefs about God.

## EVERYONE'S FAVORITE BIBLE VERSE

It seems like everyone's favorite Bible verse (at least when they're trying to keep someone from telling them they're wrong) is Matthew 7:1. The words "Judge not, that you be not judged" come from the lips of Jesus himself.

Mic drop. End of conversation—right?

Well, that works only if you scribble out the next six verses, along with some other things Jesus said and a good portion of the rest of the New Testament. In fact, just after saying, "Judge not," Jesus lets his audience know that when they judge, they should be very careful to make sure their judgment isn't *hypocritical.* "First take the log out of your own eye, and then you will see clearly to take the speck out of your brother's eye," Jesus instructs in verse 5. In other words, don't point out a sin in your brother's or sister's life before you confront the bigger sin in your own. But the whole point is to help your brother or sister take the speck out of their own eye, which requires you to judge that it's there. So Jesus isn't saying that it's always wrong to judge. In fact, verse 6 tells us to "not give dogs what is holy, and do not throw your pearls before pigs." How can anyone identify "dogs" and "pigs" unless they first judge correctly?

If there is still any confusion, just a few verses later, Jesus tells us to recognize wolves, or false teachers, by their fruit (verses 15-16). Again, this requires us to judge whether these teachers are speaking truth or deception. Then, in John 7:24, Jesus couldn't say it more plainly. He directs his listeners to "not judge by appearances, but judge with right judgment."

In Matthew 18:15-17, Jesus gives instructions about how to confront a fellow believer if they've sinned against you. (Don't forget to take the log out of your own eye first!) The apostle Paul echoes this sentiment in Galatians 6:1, where he tells Christians how to handle a brother who is caught in a sin. He writes, "You who are spiritual"—think log-less in the eye—"should restore him in a spirit of gentleness."

In 1 Corinthians 5, Paul tells the believers in Corinth that it's actually *their job* to judge other believers. He writes, "What business is it of mine to judge those outside the church? Are you not to judge those inside? God will judge those outside" (verses 12-13, NIV). Telling someone they shouldn't judge is not biblical. In fact, Scripture actually commands us to judge but to do it carefully, rightly, humbly, and without hypocrisy. And the whole point of judging one another is to protect the church and restore the sinner in repentance. It's not so that we can go around pointing our fingers at fellow believers in a spirit of pride.

The Bible tells us that we must be willing to confront each other, not only about sin but also about false beliefs about God. In fact, the New Testament insists upon it. Take, for example, the entire book of 2 Peter. It, along with the epistle of Jude, is almost solely dedicated to addressing false versions of Christianity and teaching Christians how to combat these ideas and confront those who are teaching them. Second Peter 2 begins with a warning about false teachers and the "destructive heresies" they instill (verse 1). It describes Christians who will be taken in by their sensuality. In the next chapter, Peter urges believers to "be diligent to be found by him without spot or blemish, and at peace" (3:14). Jude reminds us in verses 20-21, "But you, beloved, building yourselves up in your most holy faith and praying in the Holy Spirit, keep yourselves in the love of God, waiting for the mercy of our Lord Jesus Christ that leads to eternal life."

My bandmate couldn't rejoice at my wrongdoing. Had she simply ignored the "speck in my eye" and chosen to not judge, my life could have gone down a very different path. She judged and then confronted me because she loved me. And it quite possibly saved my life.

We can judge rightly only if we submit ourselves to God and glean from the timeless truths of Scripture. If we think we are in charge of our lives, our choices will reflect our limited knowledge, which might work out okay for a while but will come back to bite us in the end. Was Dr. Seuss right when he wrote, "You're on your own. And you know what you know. And *YOU* are the guy who'll decide where to go"[2]? Not so fast.

# 10

# FRIENDS

## You Are the Boss of You

*It matters not how strait the gate,*
*How charged with punishments the scroll,*
*I am the master of my fate:*
*I am the captain of my soul.*

**William Ernest Henley, "Invictus"**

If there is one thing I really don't care for, it's volunteering to help with children's ministry at church. I'm just being honest. I'd rather clean the bathrooms, set up chairs, or be a parking lot attendant or greeter. (Wait. Oh goodness, no. Not a greeter—introvert here.)

When I had small kids, I would wait all blessed week to drop them off in their classrooms and enjoy an hour or so of uninterrupted adult time. The last thing I wanted to do was get my two littles' teeth brushed, clothes on, and hair combed and wrangle them into the car only to get to church just in time to teach Bible stories to other people's miniature humans while extracting veggie straws from their noses. Pray for me.

But the Lord knew that my sanctification process needed this. The Holy Spirit was all like, *This is the moment we've been waiting for!* It was *because* I didn't want to do it that I decided to volunteer. I was assigned to the kindergarten class, and it actually wasn't that bad. There were a few veggie straw incidents, but mostly I just had to constantly refill snack cups to a chorus of five-year-olds politely reciting, "More please!"

One morning when it came time for the "Bible study" '(yes, I put that in quotation marks on purpose), the satiated mini people all sat crisscross applesauce on the round braided rug in front of the giant flat screen that would serve as the Sunday school teacher. The scene opened with a perky middle-aged man wearing a hat. He reminded me of a *Saturday Night Live* sketch featuring Steve Martin and Dan Aykroyd that my parents watched when I was a kid. The *SNL* piece featured Martin and Aykroyd as the Festrunk brothers, better known as "two wild and crazy guys!" The energetic father figure in the Sunday school video introduced the children to their Bible story of the day, Mark 2:1-12. Even though I was skeptical of the over-the-top sunny disposition of the host, I was pleasantly surprised to hear him paraphrase the story accurately.

It went something like this. When people found out that Jesus was staying at a local house in Capernaum, they flocked there, filling it and leaving no room for anyone else to enter. As Jesus was preaching, four guys carrying a paralyzed man were determined to get their friend to Jesus. Due to the crowded space, they removed the roof from the house and lowered him down. Jesus saw the faith they displayed and forgave the sins of the paralyzed man. This caused quite a kerfuffle among the scribes, who were secretly accusing him of blasphemy in their own hearts. After all, only God could forgive sins! Jesus, who actually *is* God, demonstrated the divine attribute of omniscience (God being all-knowing) and read their minds. He used what seemed to be his favorite divine title, "Son of Man," to describe himself and basically asked which was harder—to forgive sins or heal a paralytic? Then, in a radical display of divinity, Jesus provided the paralytic a two-for-one deal. Jesus not only forgave his sins but healed his body as well.

It's such a rich passage with so much going on. There are themes of Jesus' divinity, the active faith of the paralytic's friends, and the growth of Jesus' fame and reputation. There is also the gathering of crowds, not just to receive physical healing but also to hear the Word of God, which fulfills an Old Testament prophecy about the Messiah bringing "good news to the poor" (Isaiah 61:1). It's also one of the bread crumbs on the trail that leads to the religious leaders' growing hatred of Jesus and murder plot against him.

After the hatted man in the video relayed this story to the cross-legged youngsters, he cheerily asked them to think about the story's message before revealing the lesson's takeaway. I waited with rapt attention to hear what these future Bible scholars might bring home to their parents. Would it be the divinity of Jesus? His forgiveness of sins? The importance of faith? All nopes. The big announcement: "This is a story about how important it is to . . . [wait for it] . . . *have good friends.*" Excuse me, what?

I wondered if I had misheard until he continued with something like, "Everyone needs to have good friends to help you when you are weak or sick or can't do things for yourself. This man had four good friends, and that's why he was able to get to Jesus. That's what this story is about." I couldn't believe it. The video had taken a story about the gospel and made it into a lighthearted tale about friendship with your bros and your new BFF, Jesus.

It's no wonder Christians are so confused about what God really wants for their lives. We've been taught to read the Scriptures through the lens of self: What does this passage say about *me*? What does it mean to *me*? How can it help *me* feel better? Which character do *I* most resonate with in this story? How can I grab life by the horns, chase my dreams, and control my destiny while grabbing a few Bible verses to encourage me along the way? Essentially, we have been taught: *You are the boss of you. You can shape the meaning of the Bible to fit your own life*. It's not just kids' videos that encourage people to look at life through the lens of self.

## SELF-MADE SUCCESS?

"Rachel Hollis is taking the world by storm." This was the opening line of the blog post I wrote in 2018 reviewing one of the bestselling books in the country.[1] At the time, *Girl, Wash Your Face* had sold over a million copies, and Hollis was establishing a Facebook following more than a million strong. Her entire brand was built upon the idea that women believe a bunch of lies: "The truth? You, and only you, are ultimately responsible for who you become and how happy you are. That's the takeaway."[2] In the introduction alone she repeats this point several times. She writes, "Understanding that you choose your own happiness, that you have control of your own life, is so important" and "I want to shout at the top of my lungs until you know this one great truth: you are in control of your own life."[3] Work hard, get up early, hustle hard, and dream big. In other words, you are the boss of you.

Millions of people bought into her message of self-made success, and sadly, millions of people have now observed the fallout of that ideology. In spring 2021, Hollis took to social media to publicly vent about a comment she received during a livestream in which she was called "unrelatable" for being privileged enough to hire a woman to clean her house twice a week. Hollis ranted, "What is it about me that made you think I want to be relatable? No, sis. Literally everything I do in my life is to live a life that most people can't relate to."[4] She went on to boast that she works harder and wakes up earlier than most people. In the caption below the video, she mentioned the names of several women such as Harriet Tubman, Oprah, and Malala Yousafzai who were also "unrelatable." The post was removed shortly after a social media mob unleashed the fullness of its tweetful fury on Hollis's brand. Fans who had connected with Hollis's stories of her weaknesses, struggles, and most embarrassing moments (such as peeing her pants on a trampoline) felt betrayed by the news that she never wanted to be relatable in the first place. Others were deeply offended that she compared herself to minorities who had to overcome obstacles that Hollis never had faced.

And this was coming from a woman who had written in the introduction to *Girl, Wash Your Face*, "What if I wrote a whole book about all the ways I have struggled and then explained the steps that helped me get past those times?"[5] Hollis had built her brand by sharing how she'd overcome personal challenges to achieve her dreams, all with the intention of telling women that they could do the same. Ultimately, the new Tower of Babel punished Hollis with a swift and definite cancellation. At the time of the writing of this book, she is slowly making her way back into the good graces of many of her supporters. Time will tell if she is able to regain their trust and following. But for now, this is a sad snapshot into the endgame of putting yourself first and trying to control your destiny.

## WHO'S IN CHARGE HERE?

What's your authority? Have you ever thought about that? For some, it's their own feelings and preferences. For others, it's science and reason. For many, it's a mix of feelings, self-determined morality, reason, and attraction. Many people probably haven't even given it much thought. Seventeenth-century theologian and philosopher, mathematician, inventor, physicist, and writer (it's okay; everyone was smarter back then) Blaise Pascal famously wrote, "People almost invariably arrive at their beliefs not on the basis of proof but on the basis of what they find attractive." Pascal made an important observation about how humans tend to determine their authority for truth. Simply put, most of us aren't simply analyzing facts and coming to unbiased conclusions. We tend to base our authority for what we should and shouldn't do, think, and believe mostly on what makes us comfortable. We all have biases . . . even scholars and scientists.

Think about this. The basic purpose of life science is to discover knowledge about the natural world. Scientists do this by forming a hypothesis, making predictions, evaluating evidence, doing experiments, and ultimately coming to a conclusion. But scientists cannot interpret the evidence without doing some philosophical thinking. This is why two different scientists can evaluate the same data and come to two different conclusions. Some scientists begin this process with the belief that God doesn't exist. They assume all that exists is matter, and all phenomena result from matter interacting with other matter. This is a philosophical belief called materialism. The problem is that this theory can't be tested in a lab. Because you can't prove it, it's basically an assumption and has no category to explain nonmaterial phenomena like the soul or the existence of a nonmaterial divine Being. As a result, materialism starts by ruling God out of the picture. Physicist Paul Davies once observed, "Science takes as its starting point the assumption that life wasn't made by a god or a supernatural being."[6] University of California–Berkeley philosophy professor John Searle identified materialism as something more like a religious belief than a scientific fact by describing it as "the religion of our time." He went on to say, "Like more traditional religions, it is accepted without question and it provides the framework within which other questions can be posed, addressed, and answered."[7]

The scientist is dependent upon nonmaterial realities (like thinking) to come to the scientific conclusion that materialism is true. How's that for a contradiction? With the digital Tower of Babel fully operational, there is no end to the plethora of resources available to help you try to figure out your authority. And if there is no God, most will say it's found inside yourself. But is that true?

## THE BIBLE IS THE BOSS OF YOU

Friends, if you are a Jesus follower, he is in charge. Jesus is the boss of you, and he says the Bible is also the boss of you.

Not only that, but the Bible isn't about you. It's not about me either. It's not simply a book of wisdom to help guide us through life nor an ancient spiritual travel journal written by people who were just doing their best to understand God in the times and places in which they lived. The Bible is a book about God. More specifically, it's a book about Jesus. It reveals the nature and character of God, his plan of salvation, and the overarching history of the world from start to finish. It's inspired by God, and because of that, it's without errors, contradictions, or mistakes. I know these sound like bold claims, but I hope to prove them to you as we look at what Jesus had to say about Scripture.

When Jesus quoted or commented on the Scriptures, the New Testament didn't yet exist. So his comments were about the "Jewish Scriptures," the books in our Old Testament. So the million-dollar question is . . . what did Jesus think about these books? Did he think they were temporary, mistaken, or simply the subjective theological observations of religious people?

First, many times Jesus called the Scriptures the "Word of God." In Matthew 15:3, he chastised the religious leaders for breaking the commandment of God. He continued in verse 4, "God commanded, 'Honor your father and your mother,' and, 'Whoever reviles father or mother must surely die.'" He was referring to prophecies from Exodus 20:12, Exodus 21:7, Leviticus 19:3, and Deuteronomy 5:16. Notice that Jesus referred to three different Old Testament books and said, "God commanded . . ." He didn't say, "Ancient scribes who were figuring God out in their time and place commanded . . ."

In Mark 7:8-13, Jesus criticized the Pharisees for leaving "the commandment of God" and adding their own traditions to Scripture. He told them that they "void the *word of God* by [their] tradition" (emphasis added). Just before quoting Exodus 3:6 in Matthew 22:31-32, he said, "Have you not read what God said to you?" (NIV). Jesus continually referred to the Old Testament Scriptures as the Word of God. Considering that Jesus *is* God, doesn't it make sense that he would expect his followers to take his own Word seriously?

Jesus also indicated that the books of the Old Testament were inspired by God. One day as he was teaching a large crowd in the Temple courts, he encountered some Pharisees, and let's just say there was an exchange of words. Essentially, Jesus appealed to the inspiration of Scripture to help them understand that the Messiah is more than just a descendant of David. He said, "How is it then that David, speaking by the Spirit, called him [the Messiah] 'Lord'?" (Matthew 22:43, NIV). In fact, it's here that Jesus himself gave a definition for divine inspiration. He affirmed that David, along with the other biblical writers, was "speaking by the Spirit" when he wrote Scripture. Biblical scholar John Wenham noted that whenever Jesus said, "It is written," he was also appealing to the inspiration of Scripture: "It is . . . clear that Jesus understood 'It is written' to be equivalent to 'God says'."[8]

Jesus also declared that the Scriptures were historically reliable. He continually referred to Old Testament characters as actual people who lived in real times and places. He spoke of Abel (Luke 11:51), Noah (Matthew 24:37-38; Luke 17:26-27), Abraham (John 8:56), Lot (Luke 17:28-29), Isaac (Matthew 8:11), Jacob (Luke 13:28), Moses (John 7:22), David (Matthew 12:3-4; 22:43; Mark 12:36; Luke 20:42), Solomon (Matthew 6:29; 12:42; Luke 11:31; 12:27), Elijah (Luke 4:25-26), Elisha (Luke 4:27), Jonah (Matthew 12:39-41; Luke 11:29-30, 32), and Zechariah (Luke 11:51).

He also described events such as the institution of circumcision (John 7:22), the judgment of Sodom and Gomorrah (Matthew 10:15), the miracle of manna (John 6:31), Moses lifting the snake in the wilderness (John 3:14), and David eating consecrated bread (Matthew 12:3-4; Mark 2:25-26; Luke 6:3-4) as real history. If that were not enough, Jesus affirmed two of the most disputed Old Testament stories. Some skeptics claim that the great flood and the story of Jonah never actually happened—and yet, Jesus affirmed that both were historical (Matthew 24:37-39; Matthew 12:40). In fact, he compared the historicity of the story of Jonah with the historicity of his own resurrection, an event that the apostle Paul claimed could support Christianity or discredit it, based on whether or not it really happened (1 Corinthians 15:14)!

Jesus also introduced the idea that the Scriptures are without error. Remember the Sadducees, who didn't believe in the resurrection of the dead? Once when they tried to trap Jesus, he corrected them by saying, "You are wrong, because you know neither the Scriptures nor the power of God" (Matthew 22:29). Why would he compare their error with the Scriptures if he thought these sacred writings might have gotten some things wrong? Jesus' view of God's Word can also be understood by a statement he made when he was about to be stoned by the Jews for claiming to be one with the Father. In John 10:35, he said, "Scripture cannot be broken."

Jesus also affirmed the idea that God's Word will never pass away, a common theme found in both the Old and New Testaments. He could not have endorsed this more plainly than he did in Matthew 5:17-18: "Do not think that I have come to abolish the Law or the Prophets [the Old Testament]; I have not come to abolish them but to fulfill them. For truly, I say to you, until heaven and earth pass away, not an iota, not a dot, will pass from the Law until all is accomplished." This speaks to the imperishability of the Old Testament Scriptures. Jesus also said, "It is easier for heaven and earth to pass away than for one dot of the Law to become void" (Luke 16:17). Jesus is asserting that he did not come to ignore, deny, or oppose the Scriptures but to fulfill them completely.

Just after his resurrection, Jesus encountered two followers who didn't recognize him on the road to Emmaus (Luke 24:13-35). They were discussing how disappointed they were that Jesus had been crucified because they had hoped he would have been the one to redeem Israel. In verse 25 Jesus scolded them for being "slow of heart to believe all that the prophets have spoken!" Then verse 27 (NIV) tells us, "Beginning with Moses and all the Prophets, he explained to them what was said in all the Scriptures concerning himself." It's fascinating that the very first thing Jesus wanted these followers to know after his resurrection is that the Old Testament is about *him*. Some commentators suggest this is why Jesus kept himself from being recognized—because he wanted the disciples' faith and beliefs to be based on Scripture first.[9]

When Jesus was tempted by the devil in the wilderness (Matthew 4:1-11), he appealed to the authority of the Scriptures to fend off the attack. As God incarnate, he could have called down a legion of angels or employed any means of defense to ward off the temptation of the enemy. Instead, he chose to quote the Old Testament. When Jesus responded to the devil with "It is written," New Testament scholar Leon Morris noted that this "points to the reliability and unchangeability of Scripture. For Jesus, to have found a passage in the Bible that bears on the current problem is to end all discussion."[10] Given what Jesus believed about the Scriptures, it's so clear that he expected his followers to obey them. If Jesus believed they were the inspired, unbreakable, imperishable, unchangeable, inerrant, and historically reliable word of God, shouldn't we?

## MAKING SENSE OF SCRIPTURE

Even though the Bible is inspired by God and authoritative for our lives, it still must be interpreted. We have to read the words and understand what they mean before we apply them to our circumstances. This may sound simple, but there are actually quite a few things to consider when interpreting Scripture. First, we must understand that the Bible is not simply one book. It's a collection of books that were written over a period of about fifteen hundred years by approximately forty different authors living in various geographical locations. When interpreting the Bible, it's important to keep the following in mind.

1. **Know the genre.** Each book of the Bible has a genre. For example, some biblical writings are poetry while others are historical narrative. Some are biographies, some are epistles (letters), and some are records of law. If you read *Live Your Truth and Other Lies* as if it's a history book, you'll likely be very confused. That's because it's not in the genre of history. Likewise, if you read a biblical historical narrative as if it's a code of law, you could get into some serious trouble.

   Here's a great verse to stitch on a pillow: "Go and hide in the vineyards and watch. When the young women of Shiloh come out to join in the dancing, rush from the vineyards and each of you seize one of them to be your wife" (Judges 21:20-21, NIV). Just kidding. Don't stitch that on a pillow. When I first read this, I thought, *What! The Bible is telling men to "catch wives" for themselves?* This is where genre becomes really important. This passage is found in the book of Judges, which is part of a larger historical work called Deuteronomistic history that also includes Deuteronomy, Joshua, and the two books of Samuel and two books of Kings.

When history is being recorded, it is going to accurately record humans doing horrible things. So when interpreting Scripture, it's super important to remember that God does not approve of everything recorded in the Bible. Some passages are descriptive, in that they simply describe a certain behavior. Others are prescriptive, in that they prescribe or advocate a certain behavior. This passage from Judges is *describing* an event, not *prescribing* behavior. We'll refer back to this passage as we learn more principles of biblical interpretation.

2. **Practice good grammar.** This may seem fairly obvious, but reading and interpreting the Bible requires some grammar. For example, reading the Bible "literally" doesn't mean we *take* everything in it literally. *Merriam-Webster's* definitions of the word *literal* include: "adhering to fact or to the ordinary construction or primary meaning of a term or expression; free from exaggeration or embellishment; characterized by a concern mainly with facts."[11] Sometimes the primary meaning of an expression makes use of a figure

of speech—while still being factual. Here's what I mean. Imagine you are talking with a friend and you say, "Wow, it's really raining cats and dogs out there!" Then envision your friend retorting, "What? It can't rain animals. That is an unscientific and silly understanding of precipitation." Of course you would be a bit confused by your friend's inability to recognize this common idiom. Even though you weren't using literal language, you were communicating a literal fact: It's raining really hard outside.

The Bible also uses figures of speech such as idioms and metaphors. In fact, Scripture describes Jesus as a door, a shepherd, a stone, bread, a lion, a root, and a vine. It characterizes his followers as salt, light, branches, and sheep.[12] Unless you literally think that Jesus has fangs and claws, and that his followers have woolly coats and hooves, you probably understand these metaphors instinctively. But sometimes it isn't quite that simple.

3. **Compare Scripture with Scripture.** Let's be honest. Some portions of the Bible are easier to understand than others. The gospel? Crystal clear. The reason people were told to "catch wives" for themselves in Judges? A little less clear. This is why it's extremely important to examine a difficult verse of the Bible in light of the general teaching of *all* of Scripture and what has been revealed about the nature and character of God. In other words, it's important that we read

Scripture through God's eyes, not through the lens of our own contemporary culture.

Second Timothy 3:16-17 tells us that "all Scripture is breathed out by God and profitable for teaching, for reproof, for correction, and for training in righteousness, that the man of God may be complete, equipped for every good work." Since all Scripture is breathed out by God, it's all his Word. He doesn't contradict himself, which is why we can interpret Scripture in light of other Scripture. The whole counsel of God's Word gives us a seamless and definitive understanding of everything God wants us to know.

Now back to that pesky wife-catching verse. Let's compare it with the rest of what is revealed in Scripture. We know from Genesis 2:22-24 that marriage was originally given by God to be a uniting of man and woman into "one flesh." In Ephesians 5:25, husbands are commanded to love their wives as Christ loves the church. In Deuteronomy 24:5, the woman's happiness in marriage is valued. Exodus 21:16 forbids kidnapping, and many times in Scripture, our relationship with Christ is compared to a marital relationship. The general testimony of Scripture is that marriage was created as a loyal, intimate, and sacred partnership. In light of the *whole* of Scripture, it's fair to conclude that there is more to Judges 21 than initially meets the eye.

**4. Consider the context.** To really understand what's happening in a certain passage, we must consider the overarching view of where the particular passage fits into the book's structure and the historical context within which the particular passage was written. The surrounding context, what comes before and after the passage we are reading, is also important. Sometimes this means we have to read a chapter before and after to get a firm grasp of what the verse is actually communicating. Regarding the whole wife-stealing incident from Judges 21, here is some much-needed context:

*Overarching view:* This passage is found in the very last chapter of the book of Judges, in a cluster of chapters that describe the most lawless and dark periods of Israel's history. If they made a movie version of this particular biblical narrative, it would definitely be rated R or worse. This was an age of anarchy, and these chapters illustrate Israel's failure to live in covenant relationship with God.

*Historical context:* In the beginning of the chapter, the men of Israel swore an oath to not give their daughters to the Benjaminites in marriage. It turns out that this whole conflict begins somewhere around Judges 19, which describes how a man's concubine was abused, raped, and killed by men from the tribe of Benjamin. He cut up her body into twelve parts (did I mention this was a dark period of Israel's history?) and sent them into all the areas of Israel. This basically started a war between the tribe of Benjamin and the rest of Israel. What ensued was a brutal and bloody battle that claimed the lives of multiple thousands of people. When it was over, there weren't many Benjaminite men left, and there were no women for them to marry. Israel had vowed not to give their women to the Benjaminites in marriage; however, they didn't want to lose the bloodline of this tribe. So they took matters into their own hands and suggested the Benjaminites "catch wives" for themselves from the young women of Shiloh. They let themselves off on a technicality because they wouldn't be actually "giving" them wives.

Reader, please note: God did not tell them to do this. Neither did one of his prophets. Everything we read about the nature and character of God, as well as his attitude toward women and marriage, would forbid the Israelites from doing such evil. But of course, they were free to exercise their will, which sadly had gotten them into this mess in the first place. Knowing *who* gave the instruction in this verse is key to understanding *how* to interpret it.

The puzzle of this passage is solved by recognizing what is explained at the end of the chapter in verse 25: "In those days there was no king in Israel. Everyone did what was right in his own eyes." In other words, it was a time of utter lawlessness and evil. This is what happens when humans rebel against God. It's chilling. It's supposed to be. We should be disturbed by this passage . . . not because it's recorded in the Bible and therefore think God must approve of it. No. It's disturbing because it shows us the repercussions of taking matters into our own hands, trusting our own hearts, and acting on our inner wants and desires. Our hearts are desperately sick. This passage illustrates that in unvarnished terms.

5. **Apply the passage to your life.** Wow, this chapter took a dark turn, didn't it? Thanks for hanging in there. This material is important, though, because it highlights how vital it is to understand these basic interpretive principles. Notice we haven't even talked about application yet. In their zeal to apply the Bible to their lives, many Christians skip over these principles entirely and immediately ask, *What does this mean for my life?* However, approaching Scripture through the lens of self will lead to a flimsy view of God. Trust me. I've been there.

When I was younger, I had no clue about these principles. I would simply pluck an Old Testament battle out of its historical context and instantly apply it to some kind of spiritual battle I found myself in. I would claim promises that were not made to me and cling to them like my life depended on them. I didn't even think to consider that many of the promises made to Israel in the Old Testament weren't given to me personally. I failed to read on in these promise passages and notice that often a curse was promised for disobedience. It's easy to claim Jeremiah 29:11, "For I know the plans I have for you, declares the LORD, plans for welfare and not for evil, to give you a future and a hope," as a guarantee of a prosperous, suffering-free life. But let's take our principles and apply them (before we apply the verse to our personal lives).

First, let's consider the historical context. This verse is found in a historical narrative in which Jeremiah was serving as a prophet just before and after Israel was taken into captivity by the Babylonians. Remember when the teenager Daniel was captured and brought to Babylon, where he wouldn't eat the meat from the king's table and his friends wouldn't bow to the giant golden idol? It was around that same time. We find this particular promise in a letter Jeremiah wrote to the exiles, encouraging them to go about their lives and trust in God. The prophet assured them that after seventy years of captivity, God would bring them back to the Promised Land. (This is the immediate context.)

Now comes the fun part. When we compare this passage with the whole of Scripture, a story begins to emerge. We know that it is ultimately about Jesus, and in the context of the whole story of Scripture, we know that God promised the Messiah through the Jewish people. This passage in Jeremiah is extremely important because it's basically God vowing to keep that promise. He knew the plans he had for Israel. They were in captivity due to their disobedience, but he would restore them. His plan of salvation would not be thwarted. This situation was a part of his plan. What a rich view of God's sovereignty, a principle that we can immediately apply to our lives. God is sovereign and trustworthy, and we can rest in that.

So what is the application of Jeremiah 29:11 to a Christian today? When we place the passage in the context of what we know from Genesis to Revelation, we learn that God *does* have a plan for us . . . and it *is* a future filled with hope. However, it's not necessarily promised to us in this life (and we aren't in captivity in Babylon, so there's that). But in a way, we are *kind of like* those Israelites in captivity. First Peter 2:11, NIV, tells us that we are "foreigners and exiles" on this earth. Second Peter 3:13 teaches us to look to the future hope of a new creation. We can remember this beautiful promise made to Israel and know that the same God who led them in and out of captivity is in charge of our destiny as well. He doesn't change, and we can rest in his sovereignty, as well as his plan to bring us to a new heaven and new earth (Revelation 21–22).

## A CERTAIN DESTINY

Knowing that God holds our future should bring us comfort. I suggest we look to Paul as a great example of someone who deeply understood this. The apostle Paul was kidnapped, beaten, whipped, imprisoned, ridiculed, shipwrecked, and stoned—all before he was finally beheaded. Imagine if Paul had embraced the cultural mantra, "You are the boss of you"! My goodness, he would have probably followed his heart all the way out of being beaten and stoned. Instead, when he was imprisoned for preaching the gospel, he basically viewed that as an opportunity to start a prison ministry. We are not the boss of ourselves. Jesus is the boss of us, and he says the Bible is the boss of us. And we could spend the rest of our lives plumbing the depths of its wisdom and God-breathed truth. Pastor and theologian James Montgomery Boice put it best:

> The Bible is something more than a body of revealed truths, a collection of books verbally inspired of God. It is also the living voice of God. The living God speaks though its pages. Therefore, it is not to be valued as a sacred object to be placed on a shelf and neglected, but as holy ground, where people's hearts and minds may come into vital contact with the living, gracious and disturbing God.[13]

What a blessing to plant our feet on an unchanging authority. One that is entirely truthful. Wholly perfect and unfailing. And the great advantage of standing on the enduring truths of God's Word is that his definitions don't change. The love described in the Bible will always be real love . . . despite our culture's best efforts to redefine that little four-letter word.

# 11

# JUKEBOX

It's All about Love

All you need is love. But a little chocolate
now and then doesn't hurt.

Attributed to Charles M. Schulz

When I was eight or nine, my mom switched from being health-food hippie mom to on-a-first-name-basis-with-the-local-pizza-maker mom. And it seemed to happen overnight. For example, on my seventh birthday, she baked a nutritious banana spice cake sweetened with honey and freckled with carob chips. Then all of a sudden we were frequenting the local pizza joint when we weren't ordering delivery or driving through McDonald's. Looking back, I realize—of course—she had just given birth to her fourth child and all the prior rules were now out the window. It's like the comedian Jim Gaffigan said: "Want to know what it's like to have a fourth? Just imagine you're drowning . . . and then someone hands you a baby."[1] (I experienced a similar shift. With my first child, I used a hand-operated grain mill to grind sprouted millet and wheat berries. By the time my second was born, I was pretty much dipping the pacifier in melted ice cream just to grab a moment's peace.) To my mom, who had three young, boisterous daughters, a newborn baby, and a husband who was gone a lot of the time, pizza must have seemed like God's literal extended hand of mercy. (That, and Calgon bath powder.)

Back in those days, home video-gaming systems were rare (what are you, rich?) and iPods didn't exist. So pizzerias served several purposes: games, music, and carby comfort food. Often, they had mini-arcades with games like PAC-MAN, Galaga, Frogger, and Donkey Kong. If (and I mean *if*) the budget allowed a few quarters to play games, it was as if Christmas had come early. I liked the games, but I *loved* the jukebox—a state-of-the-art Wurlitzer Zodiac 3500. For a quarter, you could choose any song from the selected list and it would play over the loudspeaker in the dining room. My favorite song at the time was Kenny Rogers's "Through the Years" because it filled me with all the sappy romantic vibes about love that a preteen could possibly contain. I always saved one of my quarters to invite everyone in the vicinity to appreciate the impeccable vocal performance of the one and only Kenny Rogers.

One night, for some reason I will never know, the jukebox was free. No quarters required. You know what this means. I could play "Through the Years" about a dozen times, and no one could stop me. And that's exactly what I did. I must have stood at that music machine for thirty straight minutes hitting the button over and over and over. When the song came on, I enjoyed a marathon that lasted from the time we got our pizza until the time we left the restaurant . . . and it probably went on for a few hours after that.

The very next pizza night, I went directly over to the jukebox and searched in vain for my favorite song. Were my eyes deceiving me? It wasn't there. Who on earth had removed the best love song ever written? Apparently, after being besieged for several hours by the smooth and smoky vocal stylings of the country crooner, the management decided they'd had enough.

Around the time I was basking in the glory of the love song that gave me goose bumps and all the feels, I read in my Bible that God is love. I understood that on a certain level, but I also think I confused it with the emotional highs that washed over me as a result of the love-themed music, movies, and TV shows I took in. I read the Bible often, even as a young child, but my definition of love was probably more influenced by eighties rom-coms than it was by biblical categories. Because of this, it took me years to understand that God doesn't love me because I'm cute or athletic or outgoing or smart. His love for me doesn't depend on how many good things I do or even how lovable I am. Love isn't just something God does. It's who he is.

## LOVE IS THE DRUG

"It's all about love, you judgmental son of a b—." This, in its entirety, was a handwritten note my pastor friend received one Sunday after he preached a sermon on biblical sexuality. This particular pastor is a kindhearted old softy, and his teaching was delivered with the utmost care and gentleness. But still. Because he taught that God defines marriage as a lifetime commitment between one man and one woman, he unleashed a firestorm of controversy in his little community.

Just reading the single sentence on the handwritten note provokes all kinds of questions. If someone believes it's all about love, why would they cuss out a local pastor? I mean, if it's really all about love, shouldn't the writer have shown *him* some love? Or are we defining love differently than we ever have before?

Hearing about the letter my friend received reminded me of another note I read about in the book *Untamed*, which we talked about in chapter 5. The book's author, Glennon Doyle, recalls a letter she received from a woman she knew at her former church. The woman was confused because on the one hand, she wanted to love Doyle and affirm her decision to leave her husband and marry another woman. But on the other hand, her Christian convictions prevented her from celebrating a relationship that the Bible describes as sinful. The woman wrote, "I want to be able to love you unconditionally—but I'd have to abandon my beliefs. What am I supposed to do with this . . . *God conflict*?"[2] Doyle agreed that her friend would not be able to demonstrate real love if she didn't affirm her relationship and thanked her for her intellectual honesty. In her response, Doyle penned a good example of the current cultural definition of love:

First of all, thank you for knowing that you have a choice to make. Thank you for not landing on: I love you, but. . . . We know that Love has no buts. If you want to change me, you do not love me. If you feel warm toward me but also believe I'm going to burn in hell, you do not love me. If you wish me well but vote against my family being protected by the law, you do not love me. Thank you for understanding that to love me as yourself means to want for me and for my family every good thing you want for yourself and your family. Anything less than that is less than love.[3]

This definition of love is so persuasive because it accomplishes a couple of things. First, it appeals to a desire most people have, which is to be viewed as nice, tolerant, and considerate. Second, it is a passive-aggressive way to shame those who do not agree with your particular theological and political opinions. It's actually quite totalitarian in its demands. Consider the line, "If you want to change me, you do not love me." For Doyle to be logically consistent, she would have to admit one of two things. Either she doesn't love her friend because she is obviously trying to change *her*, or her definition of love only goes one way. For this view to remain logically consistent, it would have to apply to any sexual relationship someone wants to engage in, or any definition of family that one or more people believe to be true. That could get dark real quick. But that kind of love is not real love. It's not the type of love the Bible describes and commands. In fact, according to Doyle's definition, Jesus himself *wasn't loving.*

## SUPER TOLERANT HIPPIE JESUS?

Remember that section in the Gospels where Jesus famously said, "Let the children come to me, and do not hinder them, for to such belongs the kingdom of God" (Luke 18:16)? Matthew and Mark also report this encounter. People had brought their kids to Jesus, but his disciples thought he had better things to do so they tried to send them away. Jesus rebuked his friends and made the point that his Kingdom is made up of people who embody childlike qualities. Children trust easily, love generously, lack power and prestige, and have earned exactly zero credentials. Jesus is looking for guileless followers, not skilled public relations representatives, influential politicians, or rich rulers. For the record, PR reps, politicians, and rich rulers can follow Jesus, but the point is that Jesus isn't looking to cash in on their talents in order to expand his platform.

Ironically, a rich young Jewish ruler interrupted Jesus' admonition with a loaded question. "Good Teacher, what must I do to inherit eternal life?" (Luke 18:18; see also Matthew 19:16, 20). Maybe he asked this particular question to settle a bet between the Pharisees and Sadducees, who had disparate views on the Resurrection and what happens after we die. Maybe he asked it to figure out his own eternal destiny. Maybe he had just heard all the talk about children inheriting the Kingdom of God and wondered where he fit into that narrative. No matter his motivation, it was *the* relevant question to ask. Jesus responded by letting the rich man know that no one is good but God alone (verse 19).

Some commentators have observed that this could have been Jesus' sneaky way of helping the man to realize Jesus' deity. (After all, only God is good.) The kid didn't get the hint, so Jesus quoted some of the Ten Commandments—don't commit adultery, murder, steal, or bear false witness, and honor your father and mother. Interestingly, Jesus didn't quote the first, "You shall have no other gods before me" because he was saving that for later.

*Oh, phew!* The young man answered, "All these I've kept from my youth" (verse 21). Of course, it's probably less tempting to steal and covet if you're well-to-do, but this is what Jesus was getting at all along. You see, the wealthy and powerful young man had an idol in his heart. He valued something above God. (See aforementioned first commandment.) Of course, this wasn't news to Jesus, who knows all hearts: "One thing you still lack. Sell all that you have and distribute to the poor, and you will have treasure in heaven; and come, follow me" (verse 22). This made the affluent young man deeply sad because he was very rich . . . and he loved his money. The implication is that he chose his riches over eternal life. Maybe he thought, *Well, perhaps the Sadducees are right. My soul won't live forever anyway, so I might as well enjoy the life I have.* Whatever he was thinking, Mark alone reports an interesting fact. Just after the young ruler told Jesus he had kept all of God's law, Mark writes, "And Jesus, looking at him, loved him" (Mark 10:21). Reader, don't miss this. Just before Jesus sends away a young man who had rejected his offer and so would not inherit eternal life, the Bible says *Jesus loved him.*

Let's revisit our cultural definition of love: "Love has no buts. If you want to change me, you do not love me." Jesus was very obviously revealing something in the rich young ruler's heart that needed to change. In fact, he let the man walk away unsaved because he wasn't willing to give up his idol. According to this cultural definition, Jesus wasn't being loving. (This might be a good opportunity for all of us to check our own hearts. Are we going to believe a popular writer about love, or are we going to believe Jesus, who is Love itself?)

Consider another example in Revelation 2:1–3:22, Jesus' letters to seven different churches. Some interpreters have viewed these letters as offering a general and symbolic description of God's sovereignty throughout history. Others have understood them to be addressed not to specific churches but to *the church* in general. Still others have seen them as representing periods in church history. Whoever you think the recipients are (I think they were actual churches in the first century), everyone agrees the letters are relevant to the church today. In other words, the letters hit those churches between the eyes, and we find ourselves in Jesus' crosshairs as well. One of the letters was addressed to the church at Thyatira, a commercial center located in modern-day Turkey. It was also the hometown of Lydia, the "seller of purple goods," whom we meet in Acts 16:14. Other than that, we don't know much about the city.

In the letter to the church in Thyatira, Jesus came down hard on a woman named Jezebel, a self-proclaimed "prophetess" who enticed Christians into sexual immorality and idolatry. After giving her time to repent, Jesus said he would "throw her onto a sickbed" and "strike her children dead" (verses 22 and 23). But here's the interesting thing. Before he pronounced his judgment on her, he reprimanded the whole church in Thyatira for the sin of *tolerance*. Jesus said, "But I have this against you, that you tolerate that woman Jezebel" (verse 20). The cultural definition of love is fading fast, isn't it? Let's revisit: "If you feel warm toward me but also believe I'm going to burn in hell, you do not love me."

## WELCOME TO AGAPELAND

The Bible says quite a lot more about love. Jesus commands us to love our enemies. Does that mean we affirm our enemies in their unjust actions? Does it mean we don't try to change them? According to the popular cultural definition, it does. But that isn't how the Bible defines love.

First Corinthians 13 tells us that love is more important than knowledge, commitment to a cause, prophetic ability, or powerful faith. Paul wrote that if he had all of those in spades but didn't have love, he would be nothing. Wow. That means how we define love is crazy important. Thankfully, Paul went on to do just that. He wrote, "Love is patient and kind; love does not envy or boast; it is not arrogant or rude." (This is the part we all like. But hang on, it gets worse.) He continued, "It does not insist on its own way; it is not irritable or resentful." (*You mean, I can't demand that other people capitulate to my very specific theological and political views if they want to love me?*) Next Paul wrote, "It does not rejoice at wrongdoing, but rejoices with the truth." (*Well, shoot. This means that when I'm a loving person, I cannot rejoice in sinful behavior but am commanded to rejoice only when things line up with the truth of God's Word?*) According to Scripture, love means I cannot affirm someone in their sin, even if they insist that love requires that. In that sense, the biblical definition of love is the exact opposite of the cultural one.

The Greek word most often used to describe love in the New Testament is *agape*. *Agape* and its derivatives are used 341 times and are found in every book of the New Testament. It's the word used to communicate God's love for us and our love for God (Romans 8:37; Matthew 22:37). It's the word employed to command us as the church to love one another (John 13:34). It's the one characterizing the love a husband is to have for his wife (Ephesians 5:25), and the love we as Christians are to have for our neighbor (Romans 13:9). It's the word for love that Paul uses in 1 Corinthians 13. It's the word that expresses the very nature of God in 1 John 4:8. God is *agape*.

In other words, *agape* means divine love, not worldly love. Our understanding of the meaning of love must start with the nature and character of God. Since love is who God is, it's important we don't fall for a common error. We can't simply define love in any way we wish and then say *that* is who God is. We must understand who God is, and then we can say *that* is what love is. God isn't defined by our understanding of love. Love is defined by who God is. Throughout Scripture, we learn about this love. Theologian Wayne Grudem describes it this way: "God's love means that

God eternally gives of himself to others."[4] The apostle John unpacks it beautifully, telling us, "Beloved, let us love one another, for love is from God, and whoever loves has been born of God and knows God. Anyone who does not love does not know God, because God is love" (1 John 4:7-8).

## LOVE IS THE CROSS

Long before we were even a twinkle in our parents' eyes, God was one being in three persons, and the Trinity has existed in a love relationship for eternity. Jesus referred to that bond when he prayed that his followers would see "my glory that you have given me because you loved me before the foundation of the world" (John 17:24). Notice that Jesus specifically mentioned the Father's love for him as present before creation. But it didn't stop there. It continues today. John 3:35 tells us that "the Father loves the Son" (present tense).

Now that we know the Trinity has existed in perfect love from eternity, we can turn our attention to where we fit into the picture. God is love, and his love is intimately connected with his goodness. He loves us not because we deserve it but because of who he is. Theologian Louis Berkhof put it like this: "Since God is absolutely good in Himself, His love cannot find complete satisfaction in any object that falls short of absolute perfection. He loves His rational creatures for His own sake, or, to express it otherwise, He loves in them Himself, His virtues, His work, and His gifts."[5] Even though we are imperfect, he still loves us. But this would be impossible without the atonement. He doesn't overlook our sins or hate us because of them. John Stott wrote, "Far from condoning sin, his love has found a way to expose it (because he is light) and to consume it (because he is fire) without destroying the sinner, but rather saving him."[6] This is how we know he loves us.

God's love was made manifest in the person of Jesus. In other words, God showed his love to us by sending his Son as a sacrifice for our sins (1 John 4:9-10). Jesus hinted at this in John 15:13: "Greater love has no one than this, that someone lay down his life for his friends." This is where Jesus directly connected love with a willingness to suffer. The apostle Paul brought this full circle in Romans 5:8 when he explained how God proved his love for us: "While we were still sinners, Christ died for us." So we can dispense with the notion that God loves us because we somehow earned his love. It's not that God created us, saw how stinking adorable we were, and just fell in love with us. We were sinners, yet Christ loved us. Because he is love.

Once we understand that God is love and that he showed his love to us through Christ, we can love others. According to 1 John 4:19, we love only because God loved us first. True biblical love isn't based on the object of love but the giver of love. That's why we need to get the Disney/Kenny Rogers/eighties rom-com type of love out of our heads. True biblical love is neither a trite affirmation of someone's life choices nor holding someone hostage to our own politics or theology. Christian, you can pick anyone off the street and love them. Because true biblical love doesn't keep score. It doesn't expect rewards in return. It tells the truth. It believes all things, hopes all things, and endures all things. It never fails. Love is a Person. Love is willing to suffer. Love eternally gave of himself to others. I think philosopher Peter Kreeft said it best:

> Love is why he came. It's all love. The buzzing flies around the cross, the stroke of the Roman hammer as the nails tear into his screamingly soft flesh, the infinitely harder stroke of His own people's hammering hatred, hammering at His heart—why? For love. God is love, as the sun is fire and light and He can no more stop loving than the sun can stop shining. . . . True love, unlike popular substitutes is willing to suffer. Love is not "luv." Love is the cross.[7]

# CHIPS

### Girl Power Is Real Power

> What sort of world might it have been if Eve
> had refused the Serpent's offer and had said to
> him instead, "Let me not be like God. Let me be
> what I was made to be—let me be a woman"?
>
> Elisabeth Elliot, *Let Me Be a Woman*

Within a few years of graduating high school, I discovered I had a chip on my shoulder about men. I'm not sure how it got there or where it came from. Up until that point, the influential men in my life had been pretty good to me. My grandfather adored me, my dad basically thought I could become president of the United States, and the precious little dating experience I had was not too shabby either. I didn't grow up oppressed or silenced just because I was a girl. Yet every time I looked at my proverbial shoulder, the chip was there.

As far as chips go, this one started out small with little feelings of competition with men. It grew into a mild yet consistent desire to see them fail. Of course, in my mind this failure would provide an opportunity for a woman to get the job done properly. It progressed from there into outright bitterness and contempt for men. However, none of this was happening on the conscious level. It's not like I woke up every morning looking for ways to crush the patriarchy or destroy every guy who crossed my path. It was just there, balanced on my shoulder like an accessory I bought at a boutique. Pretty soon, this little chip grew into a big, heavy grudge. It affected how I read the Bible. I sought out stories of powerful women in Scripture, not because I found joy in learning about God's heart toward them but because it might be an occasion to see a man put in his place.

I read the story of Deborah, the judge, prophetess, and eventual military leader of Israel. Rather than humbly thanking God for the role he entrusted to her and learning what I could about *his* nature and character, I began to make Deborah my weapon. I delighted when she called for Barak, the commander of Israel's army, and told him the Lord had given them the victory, only to watch the warrior waver. When Barak said he would go into battle only if she went with him, she agreed without hesitation. She prophesied, "The road on which you are going will not lead to your glory, for the LORD will sell Sisera [the enemy commander] into the hand of a woman" (Judges 4:9). Oh my. I read that slowly and with venom. But it wasn't just Deborah. In my young adult life, I weaponized every strong woman I found in the Bible. Jael, Abigail, and Esther were all in my arsenal. And Mary of Bethany, who chose to sit at the feet of Jesus instead of cooking and cleaning? *That's what I'm talking about.*

Goodness, it's difficult to write this because God has done such a work of healing in my heart since then. I deeply love men and want to see them flourish in every way. It's tough to look back at my younger self and see such ugliness in my own heart. But that darkness was there. And its name was Chip.

## THROW LIKE A GIRL

Several years ago, a well-known brand of feminine products released a Super Bowl commercial encouraging social media users to employ the hashtag #LikeAGirl. The ad featured teenaged boys and girls acting out what it looks like to "run like a girl," "throw like a girl," and "fight like a girl." In the version I saw, every single one of the teens engaged in silly and caricatured stereotypes of girls flailing their arms while making miserable attempts to engage in these activities. In a follow-up video, the director asked young girls if there was anything they've ever been told they should not do because they're girls. They wrote their answers on large white boxes—words and statements like "weak," "slow," "emotional," "submissive," "girl pushups," "girls can't be doctors," "shouldn't be so ambitious," and "too pretty to play football." The climax of the video featured the young ladies triumphantly toppling the boxes, kicking them, and even hitting them with a sledgehammer. This ad series was received with overwhelming approval. *Self* magazine tweeted that it was their favorite ad of the Super Bowl that year, and it was hailed as "groundbreaking" by the *Huffington Post*.[1] The message was clear: There is nothing you can't do just because you're a girl.

The problem with this message is that it's simply not true. There are plenty of things you shouldn't and can't do if you're a girl. If you are female, you probably shouldn't engage in hand-to-hand combat with a man. (Of course, there are exceptions, but exceptions exist because they are unusual). If you are female, you probably can't bench-press as much as a typical man or run as fast as a man. You can't impregnate another person or get prostate cancer. On the flip side, there's a ton you shouldn't and can't do if you're a guy. You shouldn't engage in hand-to-hand combat with a woman or force a woman to have sex with you. You can't give birth, nurse a baby, or get ovarian cancer.

Of course, the messages written on the boxes varied in their nature. Can women be doctors? Obviously. Are women less smart than men? Certainly not. But are they generally physically weaker than men? Well . . . there's a reason they are called "girl pushups."

In our culture, to claim that there are differences between men and women has become taboo. Sadly, we've taken all the strengths that men typically possess and made them the standard of goodness and value. Because of this, women feel they need to fight like a man, compete with men in the workplace, and achieve all the things men do. But why is no one making womanhood the standard of goodness and value? Notice that our culture doesn't tell men that to be relevant, they must get pregnant, something only women can do. (I want to be very clear that I am not saying the only thing women are good for is being barefoot and pregnant. Still, it must be noted that one of the fiercest female characters in all of cinematic history is Evelyn Abbott, played by Emily Blunt in the horror film *A Quiet Place* and its sequels. She was literally barefoot and pregnant during much of the first film as she figured out how to defeat deadly aliens while raising capable and polite children in a post-apocalyptic America—all without having to engage in even one fistfight. But I digress.) Friends, we are buying lies. It's a beautiful truth that God made men and women equal in value and worth but different in role and responsibility.

Take, for example, the claim that women are "too emotional." Why do we automatically believe this is a negative stereotype that must be toppled in order to crush the patriarchy? Could it be that God actually hardwired an emotional intelligence into women because they are literally responsible for bringing all the new humans into the world? Could it be that they need to be naturally intuitive and nurturing, with sharp instincts designed toward the survival and flourishing of individuals? Instead of viewing this as a weakness to be overcome, I praise God for the beauty of his diverse creation.

Likewise, could it be that God has built into men an instinct bent toward protecting and providing? Could it be that the differences between men and women fit together like puzzle pieces to ensure that both flourish and that the whole family and society in general thrive?

I once talked with a young student after speaking at her high school chapel service. She was in tears over passages in the Bible she perceived to be oppressive to women. In particular, she couldn't understand why God had made men and women differently. Through soft sobs she whispered, "Why didn't he just make our bodies the same?" I had honestly never thought about the question from that exact angle, so I went to Genesis 1 and walked us through the creation narrative, paying special attention to what it said about women: "In the image of God he created him; male and female he created them" (verse 27). I explained to her that it wasn't just men who were made in God's image. Women were too.

Then I said, "You have a complete circulatory system. You have a complete cardiovascular system. You have a complete nervous system. But God gave you only one half of the reproductive system. What does that tell you?" Her eyes lit up just a bit and I could see the wheels turning. I said, "Perhaps God made our bodies different because he wanted us to understand something incredibly important about what children inherently need . . . a mom and a dad. Plus, I think it's beautiful to know that men and women *together* reflect the image of God."

I realize that according to our culture, "them's fighting words." But have you noticed that everything from music to movies to social media is geared toward making sure that women believe they are no different from men and can achieve anything men can? I've been particularly disturbed in recent years to watch more and more TV shows and movies normalize physical fights between female and male characters. I know, I know. I sound like a Goody Two-shoes fuddy-duddy right now. I can just hear myself saying that while ironing a lace doily before yelling, "Get off my lawn!" to the neighborhood kids. But seriously. It's getting ridiculous. I can't tell you how many times I've turned on the latest action movie only to see a 110-pound string bean of a woman (who doesn't have superpowers like Captain Marvel or Wonder Woman) beat the living daylights out of a big giant Navy SEAL . . . or a team of Navy SEALs. Typically, her toughness is highlighted by how well she can take a punch.

After analyzing several such female characters in film, theologian Dr. Alastair Roberts wrote:

> We have moved from a situation with distinct worlds of gendered activity . . . to one in which men and women are being pressed into a single intersubjective and existential world, one that was traditionally male. The result is a stifling of men, as manliness becomes a social threat and male strength a problem to be solved. . . .
>
> The fact that women's stature as full agents is so consistently treated as contingent upon such things as their physical strength and combat skills, or upon the exaggerated weakness or their one-upping of men that surround them, is a sign that, even though men may be increasingly stifled within it, women are operating in a realm that plays by men's rules. The possibility of a world in which women are the weaker sex, yet can still attain to the stature and dignity of full agents and persons—the true counterparts and equals of men—seems to be, for the most part, beyond people's imaginative grasp.[2]

That's a bit of a longer quote, but I hope you'll take it all in and read it again very slowly. It perfectly diagnoses our cultural problem surrounding all things girl power. But is "girl power" the kind of power we should be aiming for?

## APPLES

According to the Bible, human history began in a garden. God created the first human, Adam, and placed him in Eden with the freedom to eat the fruit of any tree except for one. "The LORD God commanded the man, saying, 'You may surely eat of every tree of the garden, but of the tree of the knowledge of good and evil you shall not eat, for in the day that you eat of it you shall surely die'" (Genesis 2:16-17).

We all know what happened next. God put Adam to sleep, did a little surgery on his side, and created the first woman. Eve wasn't there when God gave Adam the command regarding trees, so she most likely got her information from him. Enter the serpent. This creature, which Scripture identifies as the devil (Revelation 12:9), came to tempt Eve to rebel against God in Genesis 3. He was super crafty and opened with: "Did God *actually* say . . . ?" (verse 1). He asked Eve if God really said that they couldn't eat from any tree in the garden. Notice that, right off the bat, he misconstrued God's words and turned a positive into a negative. God said they *could* eat; Satan twisted it into they *couldn't*.

Eve fell for it. In fact, she did a little twisting of her own. Well . . . in all fairness either she distorted it or Adam misspoke when he passed God's instruction on to her, but either way, God's word was twisted. She replied, "We may eat of the fruit of the trees in the garden, but God said, 'You shall not eat of the fruit of the tree that is in the midst of the garden, neither shall you touch it, lest you die'" (Genesis 3:2-3). It's important to recognize a couple of important edits she made regarding what God had said. One was an omission; the other was an addition. First, she generalized God's original command, leaving out the specifics of being able to eat *freely* from *every other* tree. Second, she added, "neither shall you touch it," which wasn't in God's original edict. By disregarding parts of God's word and adding to it, Eve became very confused and ultimately deceived. At that point, the serpent went in for the kill. He basically told her that she wouldn't die (verse 4). This likely quelled any fear (remember the vampire Novocain in chapter 7? Where's Bella when you need her!) and made Eve more susceptible to his next move. In fact, he convinced her that God was withholding something amazing from her, and if she ate the fruit, she would become like her Creator, knowing good and evil.

When the serpent told Eve that eating the forbidden fruit would make her "like God," he wasn't *completely* lying. We know this because in Genesis 3:22, God said, "Behold, the man has become like one of us in knowing good and evil." Here's the thing—when it comes to deception, the best lies contain *so* much truth. In a way, when Adam and Eve ate the fruit, their eyes *were* opened and they *were* made like God, but God and the serpent had two very different opinions on that. The difference is that the serpent presented "being like God" as a good thing, but God knew it was actually a very dangerous thing. *The fruit wasn't something good that was being withheld but something incredibly destructive that God was protecting Adam and Eve from.* He wanted to shield them from the evil Satan was trying to introduce into God's good creation. Even today, Satan wants us to view God's commands as barriers that keep us from enjoying the things we are entitled to. In reality, God is protecting us from what will harm us.

But, alas, Eve followed her heart. The text continues, "When the woman saw that the tree was good for food, and that it was a delight to the eyes, and that the tree was to be desired to make one wise, she took of its fruit and ate, and she also gave some to her husband who was with her, and he ate" (verse 6). It's interesting that the apostle Paul noted in Romans 5:12 that sin entered the world through *one man*. Even though Eve was deceived, Paul tells us in 1 Timothy 2:14 that Adam was not deceived. And yet he seems to be the one held responsible. We just read in Genesis that he was with her the whole time, and according to Romans 5, death spread to all humans because of *him*. The Scripture doesn't tell us much about Adam's motivation, but it says that Eve saw that the fruit was "good," and a "delight," and to be "desired to make one wise" (verse 6). Genesis 3 is possibly the most fascinating section of Scripture to me, and there is so much more that could be said and explored. But the main point here is that both Adam and Eve, in their own way, made themselves the standard for truth and goodness instead of God and his word.

Because Adam and Eve chose to rebel against God, the entire cosmos was thrown into chaos. Creation was cursed, humans were cursed, and human death became an imminent reality.

The devil's formula has never changed.

## HOW TO BE DECEIVED IN 5 EASY STEPS

1. Question what God actually said.
2. Twist what God said.
3. Paint God like the mean bully in the sky who uses fear tactics to keep you from having any fun.
4. Persuade you to trust yourself more than you trust God and his Word.
5. Catapult your life into darkness and chaos.
6. Convince you that darkness and chaos are actually good things.
7. Rinse, recycle, repeat.

It's literally the oldest lie in the book.

## TO EAT OR NOT TO EAT, THAT IS THE QUESTION

Satan doesn't change his tactics—he just adapts them to the times. Same tricks. Different presentation and delivery. Here's an example:

> The way power justifies controlling a group is by conditioning the masses to believe that the group cannot be trusted. So the campaign to convince us to mistrust women begins early and comes from everywhere.[3]

In *Untamed*, Glennon Doyle follows these words with examples from culture in which she sees this happening. From fairy tales to the beauty industry to diet culture to the legal system, there seems to be no end to the patriarchy's rabid desire to keep women down. "The lesson of Adam and

Eve—the first formative story I was told about God and a woman—was this: When a woman wants more, she defies God, betrays her partner, curses her family, and destroys the world," Doyle writes.[4] After encouraging women to trust their desires and remain loyal to their inner voices, she turns the Adam and Eve story on its head:

> If women trusted and claimed their desires, the world as we know it would crumble. Perhaps that is precisely what needs to happen so we can rebuild truer, more beautiful lives, relationships, families, and nations in their place.
>
> Maybe Eve was never meant to be our warning. Maybe she was meant to be our model.
>
> Own your wanting.
>
> Eat the apple.[5]

For the average Christian, this may seem like a shocking interpretation. Blaming the Bible for helping to build a culture hardwired to control women might seem extreme; flipping the narrative on Eve changes the entire story. But this is nothing new. In 1895, Elizabeth Cady Stanton, an advocate for women's rights, published *The Woman's Bible*. Along with several other contributors, Stanton attempted to reinterpret many passages of Scripture surrounding women and their roles. In the preface to part 2, Stanton wrote, "We have made a fetich [sic] of the Bible long enough. The time has come to read it as we do all other books, accepting the good and rejecting the evil it teaches."[6] In her commentary on Genesis 3, particularly the interaction between the serpent and Eve, she wrote, "The unprejudiced reader must be impressed with the courage, the dignity, and the lofty ambition of the woman."[7]

## FROM VOTING RIGHTS TO PINK HATS

How on earth did we get from women being denied basic rights to being told to imitate Eve by eating the apple? Perhaps a little history would be helpful. Once upon a time, women in the United States were denied the vote, higher education, and property rights. Along came the efforts of the first-wave feminists who championed the Nineteenth Amendment, giving women the right to vote. They also campaigned for the right to own property, go to college, and run businesses. Good job, first-wave feminists! Many of these women simply wanted the same rights and privileges of men, while maintaining their uniqueness as females. Most of them were opposed to abortion and wanted to see families thrive. However, some were sold on the idea that for women to really be considered equal with men, they had to be able to do anything and everything men can do. These "egalitarian feminists" would become more influential in future decades.

The second wave of feminism started bubbling up in the 1960s along with the sexual revolution. This wave of feminism focused on issues like "reproductive rights" (i.e., abortion), workplace equality, and equal pay. During this time, the lines between men and women became more blurred.

In 1963, Betty Friedan's *The Feminine Mystique* was

published, and it would shape modern feminism as we know it. Friedan's book effectively convinced a generation of women that being a stay-at-home mom was an unfulfilling drag of a job. If they were feeling discontented, it was because the men got to have all the interesting careers, and they were stuck at home changing diapers, cooking meals, and cleaning the house. What once was viewed as a valuable, satisfying, and stabilizing role was now viewed as oppressive. Likewise, viewing men as the providers was seen as unfair. As a result, many women left their homes. Some left their husbands.

As time went on, this "option" of married mothers working outside the home became a necessity. Going back to being a homemaker would cease to become a possibility for many women. Then, as feminism became more and more hitched to Marxist ideas, the third wave of feminism, which started in the early nineties, began to see the oppression of women as a system that needed dismantling.

Today, if you're a man who helps a woman retrieve her roller bag from the upper compartment of an airplane, you might be called a misogynist. If you open a door for a woman, some will assume you must have been conditioned by society to think she is too weak to do it herself, so you are a sexist. In my view, the damage this does to women and girls is significant, and the devastation it brings to men and boys is incalculable. In her important book, *The War against Boys: How Misguided Feminism Is Harming Our Young Men*, philosopher Christina Hoff Sommers noted, "We have turned against boys and forgotten a simple truth: the energy, competitiveness, and corporal daring of normal males are responsible for much of what is right in the world."[8] In other words, we have turned men's strengths into casualties of modern feminism, which has made maleness, in Hoff Sommer's words, "a social disease."[9]

I think by the time Mr. Chip showed up on my shoulder, I had internalized some of this modern feminism without realizing it. I assigned the worst possible motives to men and bought into the idea that women were to compete against them instead of appreciating males for what God had made them to be. I am so thankful that the Lord yanked that poisonous root out of my heart before it grew into something worse.

More than twenty years before the famous (or infamous, depending on whom you ask) Women's March of 2017, I was hanging out with a couple of close friends after a worship team rehearsal in Santa Monica, California. We attended a small church that was home to a sweet and slightly charismatic congregation that welcomed everyone from the homeless to up-and-coming Hollywood actors. I was overcome with an eagerness to confess the rot that had been spreading in my soul, and one of my friends offered to pray for me. She asked that the root of this attitude toward men would be pulled from my heart, never to return. In a rare supernatural move, the Lord yanked out that weed before it grew into something worse. It never returned. I know that not everyone receives that type of instantaneous freedom, but the Lord granted it to me and I am so thankful. I would continue to have other struggles, but this would cease to be one of them.

## I AM WOMAN, HEAR ME ROAR

Not surprisingly, the Bible gives us a countercultural picture of who a woman is. When the books of the Old Testament were composed, the protections, instructions, and overall value they assign to women were unheard of in those times. When the New Testament was written, it was quite revolutionary. For example, in the first-century Roman Empire in which Jesus was born and lived, women were generally viewed as less valuable than men. From a social standpoint, wives were expected to be faithful to their husbands, but it was perfectly acceptable for men to have sex with a wide variety of people, from prostitutes to courtesans to young boys.[10]

Can you imagine how countercultural it was for the apostle Paul to come along in 1 Thessalonians 4:3-4 and tell *men* to "abstain from sexual immorality" and "to control [their] own bod[ies] in holiness and honor"? What culture expected from women, Paul applied to men as well. He went even further in 1 Corinthians 7:3-4: "The husband should give to his wife her conjugal rights, and likewise the wife to her husband. For the wife does not have authority over her own body, but the husband does. *Likewise the husband does not have authority over his own body, but the wife does*" (emphasis mine).

One scholar commented that culturally speaking, it was nothing special to say that the husband had authority over his wife's body, but "Paul's following statement affirming the reverse, that 'the husband does not have authority over his own body, but the wife does,' clearly pointed to a radical and unprecedented restriction on the husbands' sexual freedom."[11] This is just one small example of the New Testament's attitude toward women, but let's swing back a bit further in history to get a bigger picture of who God created a woman to *be*.

Genesis 1:26-27 tells us that men *and* women were both created in the image of God. Verses 28-30 explains that God blessed *them* and commanded *them* to be fruitful and multiply and to have dominion over the earth. Notice that God assigned this blessing and task to *both* of them. They were equal in value and worth, but they were also different. From their bodies to their roles, they complemented each other in every way.

Genesis 2 goes on to give us more specifics on the origin of woman. After creating the first man and all the animals, God brought the animals to Adam and let him name them. Then Scripture notes, "But for Adam, there was not found a helper fit for him" (verse 20). So God created the first woman. When Adam woke and saw this new creation, he broke out into the first poem in the history of the world:

> This at last is bone of my bones
>      and flesh of my flesh;
> she shall be called Woman,
>      because she was taken out of Man.
>
> GENESIS 2:23

He certainly didn't say anything like that when he was naming the animals! Already we can see the precious value assigned to women from their creation. From the language used to describe God's divine activity to the man's response and the woman's role, the Bible ascribes a value to woman that was unique in the ancient world. Old Testament scholar K. A. Mathews put it like this: "This full description of the woman's creation is unique to the cosmogonies of the ancient Near East. The Hebrews' lofty estimation of womanhood and its place in creation was not widely held by ancient civilizations."[12]

The word translated into English as "helper" is the Hebrew word *ezer*, which is used to describe Eve's role in relation to Adam. What do you think of when you think about what a "helper" is? A servant or slave? A butler or maid? We can fall into several misconceptions if we don't understand what the word meant in the original Hebrew and how it is used throughout the Bible. *Ezer* does not mean a servant, someone of lower value or less importance. In fact, it's a word God used to describe himself several times throughout the Old Testament. When David prayed for Israel's protection and God's help in their day of trouble in Psalm 20:1-2, he asked that God send *ezer* or "help." In another passage, the psalmist cried out, "I lift my eyes up to the hills. From where does my help [*ezer*] come? My help [*ezer*] comes from the LORD" (Psalm 121:1). In Exodus 18:4, when Moses was remembering how God saved him from the sword of Pharaoh, he referred to God as "my help" (from *ezer*). Dr. Mathews wrote, "There is no sense derived from the word linguistically or from the context of the garden narrative that the woman is a lesser person because her role differs. . . . In the case of the biblical model, the 'helper' is an indispensable 'partner' . . . required to achieve the divine commission. . . . What the man lacks, the woman accomplishes."[13]

Biblically, women were created to fulfill a role that is inherently dignified, beautiful, and just as important as the purpose for which men were designed. Ah, but then we have the Fall. What was created good became marred and distorted. Then God cursed the man, the woman, and the ground. Out of this rebellion against God and the resulting curses, we start to see all manner of human evil. We have misogyny and the mistreatment of women. Likewise, we see the overcorrections of modern feminism and visitations from Mr. Chip (as well as every other sort of wickedness). But the point is that these are all a result of the Fall—they are not the way things were originally created.

I know this sounds like a pretty bleak picture. That's because it is. Sometimes I think we humans tend to downplay our own sinfulness, not realizing how much our sin is an affront to a holy God. These distortions of what God created us to be are a part of our fallen world. But as Christians, we are a part of the Kingdom of God. Jesus is our King and ruler. When we become Christians, we submit to his rules . . . his reign . . . his ways. We don't always do it perfectly, but (remember that part about sanctification?) he empowers us by the Holy Spirit and gives us his Word to help us renew our minds day by day. This means that our past sins don't define us, and our true power doesn't come from our likes or dislikes, our ethnic backgrounds, or our gender.

## OUR TRUE SOURCE OF POWER
### <u>Scripture tells us that the Holy Spirit . . .</u>

| | |
|---|---|
| Dwells inside us | John 14:17 |
| Helps us | John 14:26 |
| Intercedes for us | Romans 8:26-27 |
| Empowers us to "overflow with hope" | Romans 15:13, NIV |
| Enables our understanding of the "things freely given us by God" | 1 Corinthians 2:12-13 |
| Unites believers in the body of Christ | 1 Corinthians 12:12-13 |
| Offers us fellowship | 2 Corinthians 13:14 |
| Opposes sinful desires and leads us into righteousness | Galatians 5:16-18 |
| Seals us | Ephesians 1:13; 4:30 |
| Gives us joy in difficult times | 1 Thessalonians 1:6 |
| Regenerates and renews us | Titus 3:5 |

Romans 8:11 tells me that the same Spirit that raised Christ from the dead dwells in me! As a woman, specifically as a Christian woman, I find so much comfort as I rest in the knowledge that the Holy Spirit is inside me, giving me true strength—not the cheap and worldly "power" of constantly contending with men for the best dropkick or influential career. When we reorient our minds around the biblical view of power, we find ourselves working in harmony with each other, not in competition. I'll gladly trade Mr. Chip in for all that. Real strength is not "girl power." The way to build up

girls is to help them embrace and celebrate the specific role and traits God hardwired into women, who are beautiful, valuable, and precious to him.

Sometimes such women are found in the least-expected places. But when Christ becomes the center of our lives, anything is possible.

# DEATH MARCH

## Live the Truth

Most of us will not have to die for our faith, though
it might come to that, even for those living in the
West. But we will all face moments when we will
have to choose between Christ and something
else that vies for our ultimate allegiance.

Gerald Sittser, *Water from a Deep Well*

Several years ago, I had the rare opportunity to visit a women's prison in Latin America while on a mission trip. Typically, the administrators did not allow groups, especially from America, to tour the facility and talk with the women. But because a local missionary whom I'll call Mary had formed relationships and earned the trust of the prison officials, they allowed me and several others from our organization to enter and visit with the prisoners. It's my understanding that we were one of the only groups they ever allowed inside.

On the day of our visit, our van pulled up on the dirt road and parked in front of a dusty wooden gate connecting brick walls topped with razor wire. We stepped out of the vehicle and walked past a long line of individual visitors waiting to enter. The line extended the length of the side wall and wrapped around the back. I noticed that many of the guests held plastic shopping bags filled with everything from bread and oranges to underwear and feminine hygiene products. It struck me as odd that almost all the people we passed were men, but I didn't think much more of it as I made my way to the check-in desk where my forearm was stamped with an oblong symbol covered with Spanish words. This deep-blue rectangular mark was my ticket to walk out the front door when we were finished. Though it was mere ink on my skin, the weight of its significance pressed into my heart.

We walked past several dilapidated buildings on our way to the dirt courtyard in the middle of the compound. As we entered a musty hall that connected the outdoor area with the general meeting room and living quarters, Mary began to explain how things worked in the prisons of this particular country: "Many of the ladies in here have been either falsely accused or framed for drug trafficking. Most are from this country, but there are a few women from America and the UK as well."

I stood stunned as she described the corruption among the police and the courts. We were told that one of the prisoners was an American who had come on vacation and met a man with whom she had a romantic fling. While she slept, he lined her suitcase with drugs, and she was caught at the airport and charged with smuggling. It took two years to get a trial, which ended up being nothing more than a sentencing. She was given eight years. Another woman was a reporter from Ireland who experienced a similar setup. One prisoner was simply sitting on a bench at the wrong time and in the wrong place. Arrested for suspicious behavior, she had been in the prison for years without a trial, and no court date had been set. Another woman was guilty of drug trafficking after trying to earn some extra cash while in a desperate situation. She hadn't been given a fair trial.

A sharp ache from these injustices rose up in me, and I asked Mary, "How can they be here without trial, proper charges, or legal representation?" What began as a weight on my heart turned into a sick pain in my chest that sank like a rock into my gut. These ladies were stuck here. But that was not the worst of it.

I had done some prison ministry in the States, so my idea of what a jail looks like was informed by those experiences (and to be honest, probably also by TV shows and movies), but this prison was radically different from what I'd seen. In this particular country, being in jail simply means you are locked behind the gate. You can't leave. It *doesn't* mean you have a right to food, water, clothes, a bed, toiletries, or anything else you may need during your stay. If you want to sleep inside a room, you pay rent. If you want to sleep on a mattress, you must provide one for yourself. If you want food, you are obligated to buy it. If you have children, they can stay with you until they turn eight, when they must leave.

Mary explained that many of the women had to resort to prostitution to meet their most basic needs. That explained the long line of men waiting to "visit" the ladies who would trade sex for food, toiletries, diapers, baby food, and clothes. "The men's prison is a lot worse," she soberly disclosed.

Mary knew everyone. She had spent years coming to the prison to help some of the women create a business so they wouldn't have to prostitute themselves. They made greeting cards, which Mary would take to sell at churches and other venues. She also shared the gospel and the love of Jesus with all the women. We walked past a few women with worn and sallow faces etched with a harshness that reflected their reality. Mary greeted, hugged, and encouraged them on our way into the main meeting space, where we were greeted by about a dozen smiling women. The warmth, deep abiding joy, and peace they exuded were shockingly different from the emptiness we saw in the hollow faces we had just walked past in the hallway. I asked Mary who these joyful women were. She told me, "These are the Christians." The difference was remarkable. Here, in what could only be described as a dirty and desolate pit of dirt, brick, steel, and despair, these women had real joy.

After praying with the small group of Christian women and then leading them in worship for an hour or so, we were led through another hallway into one of the living quarters. It was solid concrete from top to bottom with women crammed into small rooms, where their wooden bunks were stacked on top of each other and attached to the walls. Some of the inmates had photographs and trinkets displayed in the tiny spaces they could call their own. Some had mattresses; others slept on the floor.

After touring the sleeping quarters, we were taken up a flight of cement stairs to a makeshift communal kitchen. One of the prisoners smiled brightly and walked toward me, gesturing that I should sit down at the rickety wooden card table covered in a plastic tablecloth. I didn't remember seeing her in the meeting, and it was obvious now that she had stayed back to cook lunch for our group. A small plate of noodles covered in a brown sauce was placed in front of me. As I stared at it, I was flooded with emotion. I wondered what she must have sacrificed to serve a meal to several outsiders. I was hesitant to eat it because I knew what it might have cost her. I looked up and into her face, which was beaming with warmth and peace. In a place like this, where every woman had to scrap, fight, and God knows what else just to obtain basic necessities, she wanted to serve. She put others first. I suspect her reward is greater than I can imagine, both in this life and the next. Back in the days when I moved in contemporary Christian music circles, I dined at some ridiculously fancy restaurants. But this, by far, was the most meaningful and valuable meal that's ever been placed in front of me, and I ate every bite.

## CULTURE GONNA CULT

Once upon a time, Christians had a terrible reputation. In the first couple of centuries after Jesus' life on earth, rumor had it that they were eating flesh and drinking blood. This led some to think they were cannibals. Because of the whole "greet one another with a holy kiss" (Romans 16:16) thing, others thought they were a part of a secret sex cult. The Christians refused to acknowledge the pantheon of cultural gods, leading others to say, "They're a bunch of atheists!" There seemed to be no end to the various ways Christians were cultural outcasts in the Greco-Roman world. At times they were aggressively persecuted, thrown to the lions, and used as human torches to light the emperor's gardens. At other times they were simply considered rude for refusing to bow to the household god when invited over to friends' houses. Can you imagine the pressure? I mean, just do the little bow . . . what's the harm, right? Real Christians couldn't do it, which put them at odds with social norms. But Christians have always been countercultural. And as I tell my daughter, "Plant your feet in the Word of God because culture is always changing. Culture gonna cult."

That's the point of this whole book, isn't it? We've explored the me-centered cultural lies that not only lead to anxiety, self-obsession, and exhaustion but also contradict the way God instructs us to live according to Scripture. But how do we do so in a culture that changes and drifts further from truth every day?

I want to leave you with three practical tips for living the truth of the gospel in a culture at odds with Christianity. The women I met in the Latin American prison modeled this perspective, and with God's help, so can we.

1. **Know the real thing.** "Paul is dead," my dad told me. I glanced down at the Beatles' *Abbey Road* album cover, which sat on top of the desk my dad used in his converted garage office. It was really more of a recording studio, with vinyl LPs lined in rows above shelves packed with magnetic tapes, music magazines, cassettes, and eclectic books.

As I peered at the cover photo, which showed the four musicians walking single file across a London pedestrian crossing, my dad pointed down at the man holding a cigarette. "See how Paul is barefoot? That's why people think he's dead . . . like it's a sign," he explained.

I was about ten years old, and he was giving me a crash course in the mother of all conspiracy theories, which posited that beloved Beatle Paul McCartney died in 1966 and had been replaced by a look-alike.

"What?" I asked, puzzled by what seemed like such a silly notion. Wouldn't the people closest to him know that the stand-in was a fake? There was no way they could get away with that! I thought about his closest family. Surely if there was an imposter McCartney, *they* would know and want to set the record straight. You might be able to fool a few people who were previously unfamiliar with the looks, mannerisms, singing voice, and body language of one Mr. Paul McCartney. But you would never fool his closest friends and family. That's because they knew the real thing and would spot a counterfeit a mile away.

In a similar way, it's absolutely vital that we become acquainted with real Christianity. Studying church history, apologetics, theology, and the Bible is a powerful way to shield ourselves from the many false versions of Christianity that we will inevitably encounter. Knowing what real Christianity is means getting to know the real Jesus. How do we do that? We have four independent sources on the life of Jesus in the Gospels of Matthew, Mark, Luke, and John. In the study of history, facts for which there are a number of distinct attestations are considered to be more reliable. These four books tell us all we need to know about Jesus.

Our culture often tries to pass off counterfeit messages of what it means to live the good life. I was reminded of this when a friend and I decided to read a book together about how to live with freedom by embracing our true inner selves. It was a bestseller written by a self-professed Christian, and the author had quite a bit to say about the person of Jesus. The book communicates that in Jesus, everyone belongs. It describes God as a "crazed, obsessed parent who will never shut up about us."[1] While my friend and I were walking in a park one day, she commented, "You know, I'm reading through this book and the Gospels simultaneously. It's stunning how different the Gospels describe Jesus versus the way the book does. It's like I'm reading about two entirely different people." The second she said that I had an epiphany. When we soak ourselves in the real thing, we won't be fooled by a rip-off. We will spot the phony version in an instant.

As Christians, we must allow our perception of Jesus to be informed by Scripture rather than by emotional experiences, mystical encounters, and dreams. There is certainly a proper place for emotion when it comes to our relationship with Jesus. I get very emotional when

I sing worship to God and ascribe praise to his name. But we should not allow our subjective feelings and emotions to drive our spiritual lives. Our emotions should respond to the truth of who God is, not define what we think it is. When we know the real thing, our emotions can fall into their rightful place of response. When we unhinge ourselves from truth, we are left at the mercy of our changing emotions, moods, perceptions, and preferences.

2. **Be willing to suffer in the small things.** Vivia Perpetua was a twenty-two-year-old, well-educated noblewoman who was also a wife, nursing mother, and new Christian. She lived early in the third century in the North African city of Carthage, which had a thriving Christian community and was the key North African city in the Roman Empire. After Emperor Septimius Severus issued an edict making it illegal to convert to Christianity or Judaism, Perpetua was arrested along with several other Christians. We know her story because her diary is a rare example of an existing text written by a woman in antiquity. After her martyrdom, her story was finished by a contemporary, possibly the church father Tertullian, who was local to Carthage at the time.

Just days from execution, her father begged her to save herself for the sake of her infant child. She responded by pointing to a small pitcher and asking him if he saw the pitcher or if he saw something else.

He agreed that he saw a pitcher. She then told him that you couldn't call that pitcher something it wasn't, and you couldn't call her anything but what she was: a Christian. Something in me just rises up with delight that Perpetua refused to redefine words. All she had to do was redefine the word *Christian*. It would have been so easy! She could have said something like, "Well, the word *Christian* comes with a lot of baggage, so I'm happy to call myself something else." She could have saved her own skin with a little linguistic theft, but she refused. If only we'd follow her lead.

As these early Christians awaited their fate, they were placed in a dungeon that Perpetua described as gloomy and distressing. "I was very much afraid because I had never felt such darkness," she wrote. Her father continued to plead with her, pressing the weight of how much her death would grieve her mother and brothers, and most pointedly, her son, who would likely not survive should she die. Her resolve remained unchanged. She attempted to comfort her dad with these words: "On that scaffold whatever God wills shall happen. For know that we are not placed in our own power, but in that of God." When brought to the town hall with the others to be interrogated, she had one final opportunity to recant and spare her life. When her turn came, her father suddenly appeared with her infant in his arms, imploring her to have pity on him. The proconsul tried to persuade her to spare her father, her baby, and herself by answering one simple question with a no. Then he asked, "Are you a Christian?" She replied, "I am a Christian."[2] She records being horribly grieved as the proconsul ordered her father to be beaten. Ultimately, Perpetua and her companions were led into the arena. After surviving attacks from the wild animals, she died by a gladiator's sword. I find Perpetua's story to be one of the most inspiring accounts of Christian martyrdom in history.

Obviously in America today, there is no chance we'll be gored by a bull in a gladiator arena because of our faith. Why then am I using such an extreme example? What does "live your truth" have to do with persecution in the third century? The reality is that most Christians in Western civilization will not experience this level of persecution. For most of us today, opposition to our beliefs will entail getting a mean Facebook comment, not receiving an invitation to that party, or being called "intolerant," "bigoted," or "close-minded." Some will experience it on a slightly deeper level by being excluded from opportunities, feeling ostracized at their jobs, or even losing their livelihoods. But it's so important that we realize that, no matter the level of persecution a Christian will have to endure, we are called to be faithful and ready all the time. We are commanded to die to ourselves, pick up our crosses, and follow Jesus. Even in the most affluent and "tolerant" culture, we will feel discomfort and need to rely on Jesus every single day.

Practice faithfulness now, Christian, and you will automatically suffer in the small things. It comes with the package. Maybe you've been hiding your faith on social media for fear of backlash. Maybe you're a teacher at a school where there's pressure to put a certain sticker on your door indicating you affirm the new cultural sexual ethic. Maybe you're afraid to share the gospel with your unbelieving friends because of the assumptions they might make about you. It is so tempting to make minor concessions here and there. Much like the early Christians who felt cultural pressure to bow to the household god, we must resist the little compromises if we are to be strong enough to resist the big ones should they ever come. We must be faithful in the things that seem insignificant if we hope to be faithful when our lives are on the line.

In his commentary on Christian martyrdom, Gerald L. Sittser wisely wrote:

> Most of us will not have to die for our faith, though it might come to that, even for those living in the West. But we will all face moments when we will have to choose between Christ and something else that vies for our ultimate allegiance. The early martyrs— Perpetua, Polycarp and many others—did not in fact choose martyrdom, at least not directly. . . . They chose to be faithful to Christ; martyrdom just happened to be the result.[3]

3. **Be committed to truth no matter what.** When you become a follower of Jesus, you start to smell. Did you know that? The apostle Paul writes that when he and his fellow believers preached the gospel, God led them in "triumphal procession," and through them spread "the fragrance of the knowledge of [Christ]" (2 Corinthians 2:14). Back in Paul's day, warriors of the Roman Empire would hold these triumphal processions after a time of war to signify their victory. They would burn incense to the gods, and the conquering soldiers would parade through the streets to the cheers of the crowds. To them, the wafting incense would have been associated with celebration and joy. But for the defeated prisoners of war, the smell of the incense would have triggered intense feelings of dread over their bleak future—which would be either slavery or death. Same smell; two radically different responses.

When Paul said that "we are the aroma of Christ to God among those who are being saved and among those who are perishing" (verse 15), it was much like that Roman procession. To some, it smelled like life, and to others, it smelled like death. There was no middle ground. The gospel is like that, isn't it? It's radically countercultural.

Consider the way Jesus invited people to follow him. Rather than coaxing them with soft music and emotional appeals, he often seemed to be trying to talk them out of it! For example, remember the rich young ruler we discussed in chapter 11? He asked Jesus what he should do to inherit eternal life. Jesus didn't say, "Bow your head, close your eyes, and ask me into your heart." No. In addition to telling the man to keep the law, Jesus told him to sell all his stuff. After amazing a large crowd by feeding the five thousand, Jesus told them that they would have to eat his flesh and drink his blood (John 6:53-55). The Bible tells us that many people were so weirded out by his statement that they walked away from him (verse 66). He certainly never held back from telling people the truth. In John 4, we read how Christ offered the woman at the well living water and then pointed out that she'd had five husbands and was currently living with a man who wasn't her husband. Jesus told his disciples that if they wanted to follow him they must deny themselves and pick up their crosses (Matthew 16:24). He wasn't exactly worried about his message being seeker-friendly.

In his book *Awake and Alive to Truth: Finding Truth in the Chaos of a Relativistic World*, John Cooper points out: "In America, we tend to beg people to follow Christ. We even make it as easy as possible. We don't offend, and we certainly don't tell all of the truth, lest people may not want to follow! Jesus was not nearly as bashful."[4] Jesus didn't mince words. He always spoke *the* truth and did not try to soften the blow. Jesus knew that becoming a Christian will often make your life more complicated and sometimes bring a unique type of trial. In fact, if we examine some of the promises Jesus made to us as his followers, they are quite solemn and negative.

He promised that in this life we will have tribulation (John 16:33). He promised persecution (John 15:20). He promised that the world will hate us (Matthew 10:22). But because the knowledge of Christ smells so sweet to us, we endure these hardships because we remember the *other* things Jesus promised. He assured us that whoever follows him will not walk in darkness but have the light of life (John 8:12). He promised the Holy Spirit will be our helper (John 14:26). He promised that in him we will have peace and can take heart because he has overcome the world (John 16:33). He promised that in him we will have rest for our souls (Matthew 11:29). He promised that we will never die but have eternal life (John 3:16). He promised that one day death will be no more and all our tears will be wiped away forever (Revelation 21:4). This is why the "fragrance of the knowledge of Christ" is so sweet to those who are being saved. We know, as the apostle Paul articulated in 2 Corinthians 4:17, "This light momentary affliction is preparing for us an eternal weight of glory beyond all comparison."

Christians must remain committed to speaking and living *the* truth, because as we've already established, "your truth" doesn't exist. We must spread the fragrance of the knowledge of Christ everywhere, knowing that to many people, it's going to stink. But to those who are being saved, it will smell like hope and life and peace.

## OLD RUGGED CROSS

In a world that peddles the messages that "you are enough," "you are perfect just as you are," and "follow your heart," the idea that "you are a sinner in need of a savior" can feel like a death march. That's because in many ways, *it is.*

When I was a teenager, my parents gifted me with a tiny gold cross necklace for Christmas. I had wanted one ever since I saw Dana Scully wear one on the popular television show *The X-Files.* I wore it constantly, always aware of the gleaming wink it would give off when the sun shined on it just right. I loved that cross, the first piece of fine jewelry I had ever owned. I treasured it because it was a sentimental gift and also because it was delicate, and I've never been one for big statement pieces. Plus, it was 24-karat gold, which was a really big deal. Above and beyond that, I treasured it because it symbolized my deep belief that Jesus died for me on a cross. The necklace reminded me of the blood he shed to save me and cleanse me of my sin.

"If anyone would come after me, let him deny himself and take up his cross daily and follow me," Jesus told his disciples in Luke 9:23. I ponder this passage of Scripture quite often. I think of my shiny necklace and the glimmer of victory it represented. Of course, the first-century believers would not have seen it that way. The cross was an instrument of death . . . and not just any instrument. The cross was by far the most excruciating way to die. In fact, our English word *excruciating* comes from the Latin *excruciātus*, which means to torment or torture. But it wasn't just the most physically painful way to die; it was also the most humiliating. Crucifixion was reserved for traitors, slaves, and enemies of the state. When Roman citizens received a death sentence, they were given a quick and dignified execution—beheading. For the first-century followers of Christ, picking up their crosses was a deeply symbolic act, but it could also quite literally become a physical reality.

Recently I spoke at a women's conference held at a church. The next morning, I was interviewed by the pastor during a question and answer session at the Sunday morning services. He asked me, "Alisa, what do you think about when you think of the Cross?" The question took me aback because, in this type of setting, people ask a wide range of questions about everything from biblical reliability to scientific evidence for God to false gospels. I was prepared for a heady intellectual question, but instead, he asked me a deeply personal question about the Cross. You know what I realized in that moment? The Cross is the answer to every lie that tells me I can find everything I need inside myself.

None of the lies we've talked about in this book can exist in the same space as the Cross. If you want to be enough for yourself, you cannot have the Cross. It is the irritant that aggravates our sense of self-sufficiency, and it is the remedy that cures the defect that self-sufficiency creates. It is foolishness to those who are perishing (see 1 Corinthians 1:18). In our pride, we want to put ourselves on the throne of our own lives, insisting that our way is better. But as A. W. Tozer wrote, "In every Christian's heart there is a cross and a throne, and the Christian is on the throne till he puts himself on the cross."[5] The Cross will never be an instrument of rest until it becomes an instrument of death. So when the pastor asked me what I think of when I consider the Cross, I remembered an old song I wrote:

*Take me to the place where my soul can rest*
*Lead me to the ground where the Word became flesh*
*Show me to the tree where His blood ran dry*
*And I'll sit under its shade until the storm blows by*

*Oh the bloodstained tree*
*Where He died for me*
*I am safe beneath its shade and I'll stay*
*Until the storm blows by*

The Cross is not just a symbol of salvation. It's a place of rest. It's the answer to the exhaustion and anxiety of trying to do it all yourself. Let's just be honest. All the lies we've talked about in this book lead us to place ourselves on the throne. We want to be our own gods. Sentiments like "Live your truth," "You are enough," and "You are the boss of you" all sound nice, but they lead only to self-worship. Reader, if you and I dive down into the deepest recesses of our hearts, do you know what we will find every single time? A sinner in need of a Savior.

We all have a choice. We can worship ourselves or deny ourselves. We can choose to follow our hearts or we can choose to follow Christ. As the prophet Elijah said to the Israelites when they were double-minded about whom they should worship: "How long will you go limping between two different opinions? If the LORD is God, follow him; but if Baal, then follow him" (1 Kings 18:21). We could put it like this today: If the LORD is God, follow him; but if the self, follow yourself.

Pursuing Christ in a world that tells you to put yourself first is a difficult road. It stinks like death to those who are perishing. But to those who are being saved, it is life and hope and peace. Christian, your truth doesn't exist. Your truth won't bring hope or save anyone. You must speak and live *the* truth, no matter the cost. Your reward? As Jesus said in John 8:32, "The truth shall set you free."

Truth is a person, and *he* is your reward.

# ACKNOWLEDGMENTS

I would like to thank my family and close friends for always encouraging, challenging, and supporting me. You all know who you are.

My deepest thanks to everyone who was a sounding board, offered help, and gave feedback or general encouragement through this process: Frank Turek, J. Warner Wallace, Greg Koukl, Diane Woerner, David Wolcott, Craig and Médine Keener, Natasha Crain, Krista Bontrager, Monique Duson, and Teasi Cannon.

Special thanks to Greg Byrd, Peggy Dangerfield, Amanda Newquist, John Galloway, Lauren Stephenson, Rachel Riley, Debra Goldstone, Nikki Treadway, Jaime Murphy, Bethany Weir, Melissa Griffin, Trent Jessup, Douglas Smith, Kimberly Joyce, Femi Fenojo, Mimi Kroeber, Todd McCallister, David Wood, Shannon Coleman, Michael and Christine Yager, Eryn Eubanks, Sally Brown, Brandi O'Neal, Janet Denton, Aubrey Gingerich, Austin Dams, Phil and Beth Stoner, Lisa Gravely, Natalie Marshall, Mark Whittle, Greg E. Potoski, Steve Wille, Julie Gandia, Michael Peasall, Kirk and Janet Linahan, Tanya Reilly, Stephen Panayiotou, Darren Tyler, Brian Jones, Chad Walworth, Caroline Rees, Maddisen Coleman, Heather Aneja, Ryan Smoke, Brandon and

Carmen Standley, Mary Sutton, Kelsea Nemcek, Heidi Holm, and Olivia Franks for your support and prayers!

Ron Beers and everyone at Tyndale, thank you once again for believing in the message God called me to write. Jon Farrar, thank you for advocating for this book and for your encouragement and editing. Kim Miller, thank you for being so consistent to make sure everything I write is accurate, well-articulated, and cohesive. Kara Leonino, thanks for your help in shepherding this book through the publishing process. Eva Winters and Dean Renninger, I'm grateful for the artistry you brought to the book's design. Cassidy Gage and Katie Dodillet, I appreciate the creative ways in which you made people aware of this book's release.

And a word of thanks to my agent, Bill Jensen—your spiritual and practical guidance have been a pillar in the whole process, and I'm so thankful for your leadership and friendship.

# NOTES

## CHAPTER 1: AIRPLANES

1. A. W. Tozer, *The Crucified Life: How to Live Out a Deeper Christian Experience,* ed. James L. Snyder (Bloomington, MN: Bethany House, 2011), 15. Kindle.
2. Mental Health America, "The State of Mental Health in America," https://www.mhanational.org/issues/state-mental-health-america; National Institute of Mental Health, "Prevalence of Any Anxiety Disorder among Adolescents," https://www.nimh.nih.gov/health/statistics/any-anxiety -disorder#part_2578.
3. For background on the reliability of Scripture, see chapter 7 in my book *Another Gospel?*

## CHAPTER 2: TROUSERS

1. Dorothy Sayers, *Letters to a Diminished Church: Passionate Arguments for the Relevance of Christian Doctrine* (Nashville: W Publishing Group, 2004), 98.
2. Hillary Morgan Ferrer, general ed., *Mama Bear Apologetics: Empowering Your Kids to Challenge Cultural Lies* (Eugene, OR: Harvest House, 2019), 63; italics in original.
3. Ferrer, *Mama Bear Apologetics,* 65–69.
4. "Question 1: What is the chief end of man?" *The Westminster Shorter Catechism with Scripture Proofs* (Edinburgh: Banner of Truth, 1998).

## CHAPTER 3: LEPRECHAUNS

1. Helen Pluckrose and James A. Lindsay, *Cynical Theories: How Activist Scholarship Made Everything about Race, Gender, and Identity—and Why This Harms Everybody* (Durham, NC: Pitchstone Publishing, 2006), 40.

2. Center for Action and Contemplation, "The Cosmic Christ," November 5, 2015, https://cac.org/the-cosmic-christ-2015-11-05/.

3. All truth is objective. It's based on the object, not the subject.

4. I document many of these writers, including Josephus, Tacitus, Pliny the Younger, Thallus, Lucian, and Celsus, here: https://www.alisachilders.com /blog/10-historical-facts-about-jesus-from-non-christian-sources.

5. For further study, I recommend Gary R. Habermas and Michael R. Licona, *The Case for the Resurrection of Jesus* (Grand Rapids, MI: Kregel, 2004). See also N. T. Wright, *The Resurrection of the Son of God* (Minneapolis: Fortress Press, 2003). The four facts and statistic are covered in part 2 of *The Case for the Resurrection of Jesus.*

6. Gerd Lüdemann, *What Really Happened to Jesus?: A Historical Approach to the Resurrection,* trans. John Bowden (Louisville, KY.: Westminster John Knox Press, 1995), 80.

7. Bart Ehrman, "Questions on the Resurrection and My Personal Spiritual Experiences: Readers' Mailbag," *Bart Ehrman Blog,* March 24, 2017, https://ehrmanblog.org/questions-on-the-resurrection-and-my-personal -spiritual-experiences-readers-mailbag/.

8. Many of these theories are explained and refuted in parts 3 and 4 of *The Case for the Resurrection of Jesus* by Gary R. Habermas and Michael R. Licona.

9. Glennon Doyle, *Untamed* (New York: Dial Press, 2020), 68.

10. Jen Hatmaker, *Fierce, Free, and Full of Fire: The Guide to Being Glorious You* (Nashville: Nelson Books, 2020), 91.

11. Rachel Hollis, *Didn't See That Coming: Putting Life Back Together When Your World Falls Apart* (New York: Dey Street Books, 2020), 43.

12. Glennon Doyle, "How Glennon Doyle Followed Her Truth—and Why You Should Too," Oprah.com, accessed March 18, 2022, https:// www.oprah.com/inspiration/glennon-doyle-follow-your-personal -truth#ixzz6mCgQ8d7P.

13. Barna Group and Impact 360 Institute, *Gen Z, Volume 2: Caring for Young Souls and Cultivating Resilience*, 2021, chapters 1 and 3.

**CHAPTER 4: POPSICLES**

1. Kathryn Schulz, "The Self in Self-Help," *New York*, January 4, 2013, https://nymag.com/health/self-help/2013/schulz-self-searching/; Marshall Sinclair, "Why the Self-Help Industry Is Dominating the U.S.," Medium, February 24, 2019, https://medium.com/s/story/no-please-help -yourself-981058f3b7cf.

2. Sinclair, "Why the Self-Help Industry Is Dominating the U.S."

3. Chris Melore, "Nearly Half of Americans Think They're a Better Person Than EVERYONE They Know!" Study Finds, May 6, 2021, https://www .studyfinds.org/half-americans-think-better-person-than-everyone/.

4. Jen Hatmaker, *Fierce, Free, and Full of Fire: The Guide to Being Glorious You* (Nashville: Nelson Books, 2020), 21.

5. Hatmaker, *Fierce, Free, and Full of Fire*, 60.

6. Rachel Hollis, *Girl, Wash Your Face: Stop Believing the Lies about Who You Are So You Can Become Who You Were Meant to Be* (Nashville: Nelson Books, 2018), 30.

## CHAPTER 5: ARMAGEDDON

1. Allie Beth Stuckey, *You're Not Enough and That's Okay* (New York: Sentinel, 2020), 9.

2. William Klassen, 'Love Your Enemies': Some Reflections on the Current Status of Research," in *The Love of Enemy and Nonretaliation in the New Testament*, ed. Willard M. Swartley (Louisville, KY: Westminster/John Knox Press, 1992), 13.

3. Confucianism: Analects 12:2; Buddhism: Udanavarga 5.18; Hinduism: Anushasana-parva, CXIII; Greek philosophy: Diogenes Laertius, Vit. phil. 1.36.

4. If you struggle to believe that God understands your struggle, it also might be a good idea to read Psalm 103 very slowly and meditate on what King David wrote about the merciful and fatherly nature of God. After describing God's steadfast love, forgiveness, and compassion, David reminds us that God "knows our frame; he remembers that we are dust" (verse 14).

5. Rachel Hollis, *Girl, Wash Your Face: Stop Believing the Lies about Who You Are So You Can Become Who You Were Meant to Be* (Nashville: Nelson Books, 2018), 5.

6. Rachel Hollis, *Didn't See That Coming: Putting Life Back Together When Your World Falls Apart* (New York: Dey Street Books, 2020), 75.

7. Glennon Doyle, *Untamed* (New York: Dial Press, 2020), 75; italics in original.

8. Rachel Hollis, *Girl, Wash Your Face* (Nashville: Nelson Books, 2018), 31.

9. Glennon Doyle, *Untamed* (New York: Dial Press, 2020), 117; italics in original.

10. Glennon Doyle, *Untamed*, 128–129; italics in original.

11. Elisabeth Elliot, *Keep a Quiet Heart* (Ann Arbor, MI: Servant Publications, 1995), 20.

## CHAPTER 6: CHEERLEADER

1. *Chariots of Fire*, 1981, Warner Brothers Pictures.

2. Mark McCormack, "Authenticity: Be True to Yourself," HRZone,

September 6, 2016, https://www.hrzone.com/community/blogs/mark
-mccormack/authenticity-be-true-to-yourself.

3. "The Big Personal Values List and Their Meanings," Harmonious Way,
https://harmoniousway.com/blog/the-big-personal-values-list-and-their
-meanings/.

4. *Britannica Dictionary*, s.v. "authentic," accessed March 24, 2022, https://
www.britannica.com/dictionary/authentic.

5. Lisa Capretto, "Why Brené Brown 'Abandoned' the Church—and Why
She Went Back," *HuffPost*, October 16, 2015, https://www.huffpost.com
/entry/brene-brown-church_n_56200e7be4b069b4e1fb6e7a.

6. Brené Brown, *Braving the Wilderness* (New York: Random House, 2017),
40.

7. Jen Hatmaker, *Fierce, Free, and Full of Fire: The Guide to Being Glorious You*
(Nashville: Nelson Books, 2020), 8.

8. Wayne A. Grudem, *Systematic Theology: An Introduction to Biblical
Doctrine* (Grand Rapids, MI: Zondervan Academic, 2020), 204.

9. Jen Hatmaker, *Fierce, Free, and Full of Fire* (Nashville: Nelson Books,
2020), xiv.

10. Kathy Koch, *8 Great Smarts: Discover and Nurture Your Child's Intelligences*
(Chicago: Moody Publishers, 2016), 203.

11. Louis Berkhof, *Systematic Theology: New Combined Edition* (Grand Rapids,
MI: Eerdmans, 1938, 1996), 73.

12. Berkhof, *Systematic Theology*, 73.

13. Charles C. Ryrie, *Basic Theology: A Popular, Systematic Guide to
Understanding Biblical Truth* (Chicago: Moody Publishers, 1999), 442,
Kindle.

14. Ryrie, *Basic Theology*, 265, Kindle.

15. John R. W. Stott, *The Letters of John: An Introduction and Commentary*,
vol. 19, 2nd ed. (Downers Grove, IL: IVP Academic, 1988), 79.

16. For a great resource on purpose and calling, see Teasi Cannon, *Lord,
Where's My Calling? When the Big Question Becomes a Big Distraction* (self
-pub., 2021).

**CHAPTER 7: NEW YORK**

1. Bob Dylan, *Chronicles*, vol. 1 (New York: Simon & Schuster, 2011), 4,
Kindle.

2. Stephenie Meyer, *Breaking Dawn* (New York: Little, Brown & Co., 2008),
281.

3. Peter Kreeft, *Fundamentals of the Faith: Essays in Christian Apologetics* (San
Francisco: Ignatius Press, 1988), 160. See also https://www.peterkreeft.
com/topics/heaven.htm.

4. Jen Hatmaker, *Fierce, Free, and Full of Fire: The Guide to Being Glorious You* (Nashville: Nelson Books, 2020), 113.

5. Rachel Hollis, *Girl, Wash Your Face: Stop Believing the Lies about Who You Are So You Can Become Who You Were Meant to Be* (Nashville: Nelson Books, 2018), 71.

6. For more on what is called "the argument from desire," see Peter Kreeft, "The Argument from Desire," PeterKreeft.com, https://www.peterkreeft. com/topics/desire.htm. Find more on his explanation and defense of the argument here: https://www.peterkreeft.com/audio/23_desire.htm.

## CHAPTER 8: MOSQUITOES

1. Craig Keener and Médine Moussounga Keener, *Impossible Love: The True Story of an African Civil War, Miracles, and Hope against All Odds* (Minneapolis: Chosen, 2016), 170.

2. Keener and Keener, *Impossible Love*, 163.

3. Christian Smith, *Soul Searching: The Religious and Spiritual Lives of American Teenagers* (New York: Oxford University Press, 2005), 162–163.

4. Ellen Vaughn, *Becoming Elisabeth Elliot* (Nashville: B&H Publishing Group, 2020), xiv.

5. Matthew G. Aragones, "How to Stop Talking Nonsense: The Myth of Redemptive Suffering," *Patheos*, May 3, 2020, https://www.patheos. com/blogs/suspendedinherjar/2020/05/the-myth-of-redemptive -suffering/#disqus_thread.

6. Rachel Hollis, *Girl, Wash Your Face: Stop Believing the Lies about Who You Are So You Can Become Who You Were Meant to Be* (Nashville: Nelson Books, 2018), xi.

7. Rachel Hollis, *Girl, Stop Apologizing: A Shame-Free Plan for Embracing and Achieving Your Goals* (Nashville: Nelson Books, 2019), xix.

8. Rod Dreher, *Live Not by Lies* (New York: Sentinel, 2020), 194.

9. Oswald Chambers, *My Utmost for His Highest*, November 5, https:// utmost.org/partakers-of-his-suffering/.

10. Chambers, *My Utmost for His Highest*, November 5.

## CHAPTER 9: MCJUDGYPANTS

1. Rachel Hollis, *Girl, Wash Your Face: Stop Believing the Lies about Who You Are So You Can Become Who You Were Meant to Be* (Nashville: Nelson Books, 2018), 40; italics added.

2. Dr. Seuss, *Oh, the Places You'll Go!* (New York: Random House, 1990), 2.

## CHAPTER 10: FRIENDS

1. Alisa Childers, "Girl, Wash Your Face? What Rachel Hollis Gets Right . . . and Wrong," AlisaChilders.com, September 3, 2018,

https://www.alisachilders.com/blog/girl-wash-your-face-what-rachel
-hollis-gets-rightand-wrong.

2. Rachel Hollis, *Girl, Wash Your Face: Stop Believing the Lies about Who
You Are So You Can Become Who You Were Meant to Be* (Nashville: Nelson
Books, 2018), xi.

3. Hollis, *Girl, Wash Your Face*, xii, xiv.

4. E! News, "Rachel Hollis Issues Apology after Privilege Video Backlash,"
YouTube, April 6, 2021, https://www.youtube.com/watch?v=f8ws0FmAsHc.

5. Hollis, *Girl, Wash Your Face*, xvi.

6. Paul Davies, *The Fifth Miracle: The Search for the Origin and Meaning of
Life* (New York: Simon & Schuster, 1999), 28.

7. John Searle, *Mind: A Brief Introduction* (New York: Oxford University
Press, 2004), 48.

8. John Wenham, *Christ and the Bible*, 3rd ed. (Eugene, OR: Wipf & Stock,
2009), 28.

9. John MacArthur, *Truth Matters* (Nashville: Thomas Nelson, 2004), 5.

10. Leon Morris, *The Gospel according to Matthew*, Pillar New Testament
Commentary (Grand Rapids, MI: Eerdmans, 1992), 74.

11. Merriam-Webster.com, s.v., "literal," https://www.merriam-webster.com
/dictionary/literal.

12. John 10:9; John 10:11; Mark 12:10; John 6:35; Revelation 5:5; John 15:1;
Matthew 5:13-14; John 15:5; John 10:11.

13. James Montgomery Boice, *Foundations of the Christian Faith* (Downers
Grove, IL: InterVarsity Press, 1986), 48.

**CHAPTER 11: JUKEBOX**

1. Jim Gaffigan, "4 Kids/Home Birth," YouTube, April 16, 2020,
https://www.youtube.com/watch?v=-Jf2IGylAhE.

2. Glennon Doyle, *Untamed* (New York: Random House, 2020), 249,
Kindle.

3. Doyle, *Untamed*, 249, Kindle.

4. Wayne A. Grudem, *Systematic Theology: An Introduction to Biblical
Doctrine* (Grand Rapids, MI: Zondervan, 1994), 199.

5. Louis Berkhof, *Systematic Theology: New Combined Edition* (Grand Rapids,
MI: Eerdmans, 1938, 1996), 71.

6. John R. W. Stott, *The Letters of John: An Introduction and Commentary*,
vol. 19 (Downers Grove, IL: InterVarsity Press, 1964, 1988), 161.

7. Peter Kreeft, *Making Sense Out of Suffering* (Ann Arbor, MI: Servant
Books, 1986), 136, 138.

# NOTES

## CHAPTER 12: CHIPS

1. Jillian Berman, "Why That 'Like a Girl' Super Bowl Ad Was So Groundbreaking," *Huffington Post*, February 3, 2015, https://www.huffpost.com/entry/always-super-bowl-ad_n_6598328.
2. Alastair Roberts, "Why We Should Jettison the 'Strong Female Character,'" Mere Orthodoxy, April 18, 2016, https://mereorthodoxy.com/why-we-should-jettison-the-strong-female-character/?fbclid=IwAR0jHYbJO_UaPyukhmiWqOqHti8UG-9ZlYtG2vWBNTwKhhK7x4vWtMvHaG0#more-127342.
3. Glennon Doyle, *Untamed* (New York: Random House, 2020), 114–115.
4. Doyle, *Untamed*, 115.
5. Doyle, *Untamed*, 121–122.
6. Elizabeth Cady Stanton, *The Woman's Bible* (n.p.: 1898), 61.
7. Stanton, *The Woman's Bible*, 5.
8. Christina Hoff Sommers, *The War against Boys: How Misguided Feminism Is Harming Our Young Men* (New York: Simon and Schuster, 2013), 3.
9. Christina Hoff Sommers, *The War against Boys*, 73.
10. Larry W. Hurtado, *Destroyer of the Gods: Early Christian Distinctiveness in the Roman World* (Waco, TX: Baylor University Press, 2016), 157.
11. Roy E. Ciampa and Brian S. Rosner, *The First Letter to the Corinthians*, Pillar New Testament Commentary (Grand Rapids: Eerdmans, 2010), 280–281. Quoted in Paul Carter, "5 Surprising Things the Bible Says about Sex," The Gospel Coalition Canadian Edition, August 15, 2018, https://ca.thegospelcoalition.org/columns/ad-fontes/5-surprising-things-that-the-bible-says-about-sex/.
12. Kenneth A. Mathews, *Genesis 1–11:26*, The New American Commentary, vol. 1A (Nashville: Broadman & Holman, 1996), 212.
13. Mathews, *Genesis 1–11:26*, 214.

## CHAPTER 13: DEATH MARCH

1. Jen Hatmaker, *Fierce, Free, and Full of Fire: The Guide to Being Glorious You* (Nashville: Nelson Books, 2020), 11.
2. Philip Schaff, ed., *The Complete Ante-Nicene & Nicene and Post-Nicene Church Fathers Collection: 3 Series, 37 Volumes, 65 Authors, 1,000 Books, 18,000 Chapters, 16 Million Words* (London: Catholic Way Publishing, 2014), loc. 61831 of 662192, Kindle.
3. Gerald L. Sittser, *Water from a Deep Well* (Downers Grove, IL: InterVarsity Press, 2007), 47–48.
4. John L. Cooper, *Awake and Alive to Truth: Finding Truth in the Chaos of a Relativistic World* (np: Cooper Stuff Publishing, 2020), 94.
5. A. W. Tozer, *The Radical Cross* (Chicago: Moody Publishers, 2015), 138.

# ABOUT THE AUTHOR

**Alisa Childers** is the author of *Another Gospel?*, a book in which she describes the years-long journey she took as she wrestled with questions that struck at the core of the Christian faith and found the truth. She is a wife, mom, author, podcaster, blogger, speaker, and worship leader. She was a member of the award-winning CCM recording group ZOEgirl. She is currently a respected speaker at apologetics and Christian worldview conferences, as well as the host of her popular YouTube channel. Alisa's story was featured in the documentary *American Gospel: Christ Crucified*. She has been published at The Gospel Coalition, Crosswalk, The Stream, For Every Mom, *Decision* magazine, and The Christian Post, and her blog post "Girl, Wash Your Face? What Rachel Hollis Gets Right . . . and Wrong" received more than one million views.

You can connect with Alisa online at alisachilders.com.